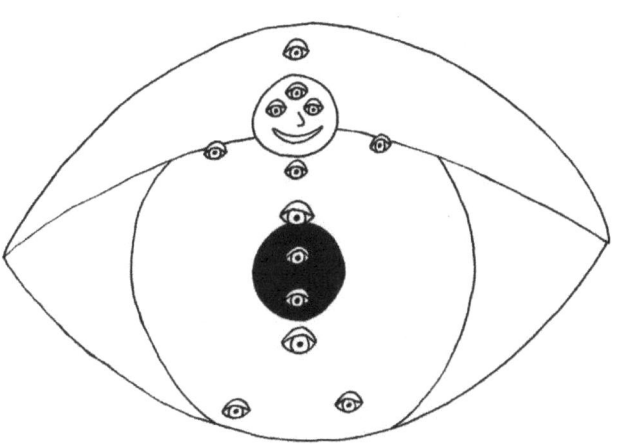

Ruminations of the Universe

Ruminations of the Universe

Enlightenment
Super Channeling
Transcendence
Enlightenment 2

by Christopher Moors

Copyright 2008 by Christopher Moors

All rights reserved. No part of this book may be used or reproduced in any manner whatsoever without written permission, except in the case of brief quotations embodied in critical articles or reviews.

ISBN-10: 0985697954
ISBN-13: 978-0-9856979-5-2

Published 2008 by the Creative Cosmos

Printed in the United States of America

Dedicated to awakening souls throughout the world,

Have courage in moments of darkness,
Persevere when difficulties arise,
Remember the whole glorious story.

Every dream is true.

Table of Contents

Enlightenment: 1

Super Channeling: 67

Transcendence: 137

Enlightenment 2: 221

x

Enlightenment

Enlightenment
A Phoenix Rises from Psychic Crucifixion

It has been 40 days and 40 nights in the spiritual desert my friends, but at last I have returned.

Many demons came out to play while I was away. With big smiles and pretty words they dance around and shout, "Look at me!" They couldn't conceive of anything more important than the flapping of their jawbone. Speaking endless lies, they accrue so much karma that it will take lifetimes to even reach equilibrium again. Burning with pain they project it in the strangest of ways. Believing exactly the opposite of reality (a by-product of Denial) they seek to push this on any within reach. When the light stands its ground in truth, they shriek and the fireworks really begin!

Seeking your greatest weaknesses, Deniers may offer riches and great illusions if only you would step into their pain trap. Everything could be yours…..ah fool….there is no intermediary between each of us and our Father's Kingdom. Within our Mother's Garden we are protected and Loved as we are with no need for any bad feeling. This deep understanding protects us from the deception of those who seek to unduly influence another on their path. We build our own personal way drawing from every tradition:

religious, artistic, literary, musical, etc.… Anything that awakens is holy.

Before Gandalf the Grey became Gandalf the White he was pulled into the Abyss. There is a certain inevitable gravity to this emptiness. Ye on the path, take heed, for one day you too will face this threshold. Everything will be taken from you and you will die a psychic death which is much more terrible than a physical one. This isn't usually mentioned because who would want that? It is like a surgery being performed on your Soul….as if you had cancer and it was being ripped right off. Ego is the cancer; the distortion of running Experience through Mind. Get past personal desires and lexicon, or there will be a part of you lost never to return.

When Aslan the Mighty Lion got stabbed to death in the place of another, He was demonstrating what always happens to those who take responsibility. Pillars of fortitude amidst an ocean of compromise, they take it upon themselves to live the truth. The truth never dies so any aligned with the truth will never die. A body is easily replaced if the aura behind it can remain intact. Certain peculiarities associated with the past body will remain with the corpse, while the new body will shine with ever more refined glory.

Enlightenment

The people often take revenge on One who comes in Truth because they can't stand to have their own flaws revealed. The One reveals them simply by existing in a state of purity. Wherever the One moves, secrets can not hide. Some embrace this blessing, some try to stop the One by Force, and others simply run away. The Forceful will blame the One as if the One is causing what they have never faced. The One could say to the Forceful, "Hey you are the one encumbering me," but instead usually goes with Compassion, knowing how sad and lonely the Forceful are underneath it all.

Alone we can not find every little nook and cranny of pain and past to heal inside. If your Heart is true, Angels and Guides, working with God and your Soul Self, will construct a scenario that will evoke in you what you need to learn to be free. Sometimes (and particularly if you consider yourself spiritually advanced), it will take a very extreme situation to bring the buried lesson front and center. These lessons can also take place in your sleep as well. If you are completely identified with your dream, you will act as you would in the body on Earth. This time lived is reality every bit as much as anything else.

Beyond anything my friends, stay the course and have Faith that no matter how messed up things get, there is a way. Never lose heart through this process as Intuition brings you closer and closer to the Center of the Sun. When you arrive, it will burn like nothing else you have ever felt. When you finally emerge there is just quiet, like a morning in the middle of nowhere. Little by little you move around and realize that you still Exist. It feels different, but you are still there. Free of Ambition and any need to do anything but serve your purpose, the fire rises, but in a new way.

It is the nature of the Sun's Son to be Courageous. Conscious and in a new body, the resurrection carries the best of what was into the new and infuses it with the possibilities of the now. Every option is available and whenever the Phoenix seeks to fly, the Lord will be with Him. It always was this way, but now He knows. Peril has sharpened His sensibilities, and Dying has given Him Life.

Enlightenment
Changes are Coming

Ye must not allow complacency to set in, or when the next change arrives, you will be caught unaware. This will in turn cause you to act in a way that is not in your or anybody else's best interest. It is resistance to the inevitable unfolding of life that causes the most suffering. These days, people seem desperate to maintain status quo at all costs; this is what causes the Armageddon feeling when the intrinsically unsustainable is no longer able to be upheld. Delay and denial cause a crash to be felt rather than a smooth progression. One cannot borrow from the future to pay for today. The day of reckoning will arrive.

Even the most lucid of us are human and feel pain when our hopes and dreams reveal themselves to be illusions that can never materialize because there is no such thing as tomorrow. Past is fairly easy to understand, but giving up ambition is anathema to most human being's latent intentions. Perhaps it is only when the Universe itself proves to us personally that it has its own way, will we be able to let go. Attachments come in persons, places, and things, while life is moving, dynamic, and flows irresistibly towards the Great Ocean.

There is simplicity beyond demons, dragons, and astral reality. It is said in Zen that in the end the Rivers will become Rivers again and the Mountains will once more be Mountains. Before embarking upon the path, the human sees such a small world. Then when entering into the inner realms, they become all stirred up and the amazing, weird, and intense amount of input and intricacies can become so overwhelming that they color their perceptions in another more subtle and elusive way. Eventually we can transcend and let go of even the most spectacular of experiences; quietness comes and you see with steady and clear awareness.

We have so much to go through here on Earth. Some don't even have the time or luxury to read such expressions as this. They are too busy running from bombs they can't see, or trying to find a drink of uranium laced water. Be in tune with your blessings and send Love to your brothers and sisters. Body, Emotion, Mind, and Soul are One and I am ever your friend.

Enlightenment
Welcome Warmth into your Heart

Welcoming warmth into your heart, the mental sharpness that proves itself correct dissipates like a shadow scurrying from the rising sun. What seemed to be inevitable is lifted to a place that includes all that was, but illuminates the pathways to reveal yet more than could have been preconceived. All is as it should be; growth and change are intrinsic to this evolving perfection.

Perhaps a flood of rationalizations come to mind as to why everything should stay the same. If this is so, consider why a simple new thought could not be entertained without an inclination to protect the old. We can add and add and add new ideas, riding this electric wave to greener pastures of power and peace.

Isn't it beautiful to wear your own skin? A certain amount of trauma is part of the experience of incarnating. We all knew that when we reached our goal, the wounds would heal to reveal wisdom. One might arrive at the ultimate destination a little sooner than another; a caring soul lends a hand. There is no rush because the river flows in its time.

The rubato of life's composition allows for all varieties to have their say. Depth and sincerity are the by-products of lessons learned. Why scratch only your own back, when a room full of scratched backs makes everyone happy? It is less effort to help one another than it is to block each other's way. Let the real celebration begin today.

Enlightenment
Leave it All Behind

We need to be free of politics and religion (including New Age) to be healthy. Never substitute one state of insanity for another. If you are intelligent, you may even go crazier and crazier in your rationalizations and your amazing universes will create heavenly prisons for you that are so hard to see that you will die never knowing what mischief your subconscious hath wrought. Oh yes you are wonderful and God's child, but that doesn't mean you sit in some kind of stupor with a goofy smile on your face basking in the glow of your own elegance all day.

There is an utterly down-to-Earth quality about the really real. It is like a slap in the face followed by a period of time for the shock to wear off. Then, there is no disturbance. Yes there remains the false and the true. Some have devoted themselves to pushing the truth, but if it is the truth only in a limited realm, you are digging yourself a deeper and deeper personal hole. You may send a wave of difference out there to slow down and reveal the false, but beware of becoming like your enemy in your aggressiveness.

Those of you who neither speak truth nor lies and simply zone out to the hum of your habits, the previous observations do not apply to you. You are more like ghosts than people. Shadows with occasional hints of a dull glow when some aberrant phenomenon happens to cross your path, you float around grooving to the beat of the same damn tune day after day. Celebrating death you flock around because it reminds you (though dimly) of the life you aren't living. Seeing the reflection of what you secretly desire you move towards it knowing that it won't shake your complacency like the inconvenience of Life and Awareness.

As soon as an individual begins to become Conscious, they are beset with a whole new set of circumstances. Suddenly you notice that you are walking amongst ghosts and that people you have always Loved and cared about are trying to convince you to tow the Party line. Like drones they reinforce the status quo in every situation. Frowning when you talk about something uncomfortable, getting angry when you bring up simple clear points, and fearing you when you give them Love they are like photo negatives who in themselves truly do not understand what is happening around them.

Controllers prey upon ignorance by pushing the buttons that activate the mind. Those not free of the mind are not a threat to them at all. They are machines that obey command orders without question. *"Yes TV, I know what you mean. I will take your talking points and repeat them to my work colleagues thinking to myself that I am informed about political affairs. With no historical background and no understanding of human psychology I declare myself an expert because I adopt the tone of my masters whom I dare not question."*

Walking just a little further, we leave it all behind.

Ruminations of the Universe

Enlightenment
Share Love with All Creation

With images representing all of history whirling before our eyes, we live at once all human experience. This is the threshold of our passing into a new era. How we come to terms with what has occurred will largely decide the direction of our evolution. Where there is war, surround it with peace and relentlessly beat the drum of destiny. We are meant to celebrate life together, but so many can not forgive themselves or each other for what they've done. That is why Jesus says, father forgive them for they know not what they do. Father knows well that younger souls are ignorant of their responsibility because unconsciousness is built into the system. Forgiveness is part of awakening and available for all intrinsically in the Universe. For a long time people creep along until they get a moment where their illusions stare them in the face. Then they can decide whether or not to admit that their life up to this point had been a distraction from their true purpose which is to share Love with All Creation.

There is not always a right or wrong way to do something. It is more important what you decide you want to do with your life. You can bark up old trees and beat your head against the wall while you secretly pine away to do something you truly enjoy or you can make the leap of faith. Perhaps there is an incredibly interesting and intricate road that leads you to your destination. Perhaps this destination is but a stop on the journey. Perhaps the journey never ends. By the way, have you ever ridden on one of the astral trains? You can meet just about anybody on one. Many of us have ridden there during our dreams while our human body is sleeping.

The universe has laws, but do not think that even they are absolute. If there is anything true about this Universe, it is that it is ever-changing. Let me contribute this to the history of science…there will always be exceptions/distortions/things-that-don't-quite-add-up because that is a quirk of this Universe. You could almost call it a sense of divine humor. Never forget the comedy that is this Existence. Look for rips and tears in the fabric of space/time, because they are there. There are even now humans on your Earth with the capacity to leave the planet. Advanced space craft sit in underground hangars across the globe while the war movie keeps everybody paralyzed in fear. Pills dull the pain though….right? They are not "bad" drugs like that nasty medical marijuana. Society can't yet let the cancer patients have relief because pretty soon other people would want some. Then everybody would start asking too many questions from the consciousness opening effects of the drug like in the '60s. Then a show of force against the people would be necessary like the various assassinations that stare glaringly back at us from the face of post WWII American politics.

Today, the average person is getting beaten down economically until they no longer have a will to resist. The people could subvert this form of control by taking the initiative to move towards a simpler lifestyle. Much of the excess that creeps in ends up being more of a psychic burden than a joy. Sure luxury is nice, but freedom is even better. This is another reason why the ways of the Eastern Wisdom traditions must be incorporated into Western Culture. This will give rise to a modern spirituality which accepts life. There will be as many ways to express this as there are people who share in the experience. Creativity will blossom and problems will be solved. Stresses will be dissolved because they won't be caused in the first place. Hearts open and intuition is heard. Happiness is the result of peace which comes from the fulfillment of your nature.

Ruminations of the Universe

Enlightenment
Question the Fundamentals

In any typical gathering of American adults you will find a group that does indeed care about their world and at least how their local universe is affected by the macro's machinations. Baby Boomers and their related "Baby Boomer Jr." early 40 something'ers, often do not seem to have the ability or desire to think past the details however. Hopelessly hoodwinked, the false premise they have been fed is seen as a cornerstone of who they believe themselves to be! Don't you dare question it or else major confrontation will ensue. The war-like qualities of their overlords are suddenly prevalent in the angry face of one whose repetitious rhetoric is easily dismantled with a shred of understanding.

In this typical group, a conversation inevitably ensues. The parameters of discussion are often set by the talking points of the leg-less bodies jabbering at the corporate news centers. This proves that for many, the news agencies are defining reality. Most people do not look very deeply into the historical/philosophical context to what is occurring. They just look at the recently defined surface, stripped of any complications. Now are you for or against? This then locks one in to the faulty premise and whatever thoughts follow run through this first basic gateway. A room full of people with the first thought gateway will reinforce to each other subconsciously that this is reality because none of them will stray from the program.

This is where the Zen Stick comes in. Of course Christians don't like it when you mock the ridiculousness of their fear based hell/guilt ruminations. If you are following the 10 commandments, you must also accept the absurdity of the Old Testament God and His childish demands. If you like your politicians so much, Dem. or Rep., do you accept personal responsibility for supporting what they represent. Are you ready to realize that your vote puts blood on your hands? There is a write in section to most ballots. Can not the human mind conceive of anything new anymore? I'd rather write in myself as president than support the preset limitations of the illusion of choice. Now that is a vote that makes a difference!

Historical certainty unravels as soon as you peak around the corner. In the past, every moment changed into another just like it does now. The mind interprets in specific chunks, but the events happened fluidly. Over many years the tale is told again and again and perceived through the filters of countless cultures. Really all we can be sure of is that people were here in the past and were much like us. The multitudes bitch, while a precious few struggle to pull their heads above the morass for a priceless view of life. Oh yes, and there are the controllers. If they are large scale or small, they are much the same. Ignorant of truth and full of self, they insult humanity again and again, completely oblivious to the karmic repercussions.

It is simply not necessary to hold on to any old ideas. We can have access to everything and the freedom to choose moment to moment. We need to learn more about ourselves and then our outer actions will not be so reckless. Destruction becomes Creation when Spiritual Alchemy takes hold. Getting beyond mind where all dogmas exist is something many do not yet realize we can do. Slip out of the mental straight jacket and unfurl your heavenly wings. Many dream of flying because they are remembering astral flights through the cosmos. You came here only for a visit. You can leave any time you choose to disassociate yourself with the context of this incarnation game.

Ruminations of the Universe

Enlightenment
Know Who You Aren't

Knowing who you aren't, is just as beneficial as knowing who you are. Try a backwards search. Every little bit you can find out about yourself will serve you on your journey. Look at all the things people do in this world. Some dive deep in the sea, and some fly high in the clouds. Others simply like to keep their feet on the ground and philosophize all day. There are people who paint and people who do heavy construction work. Some grow food and others teach our youth. What is your purpose for incarnating on this blue-green ball of life? What isn't?

Feel deeply your inclinations. Without considering this question beforehand you may have gotten yourself into a situation that doesn't line up with your natural tendencies. If this is the case, change will have to be made if you seek to integrate the soul with the body. For others not bound in this way, it will be easier. The end result for all will be harmony between what feels right internally and the external circumstance. We can go about this alignment in many ways. Notice positive attributes, such as, "I like to cook," and negative such as, "I really dislike heights".

The essential component to the whole process is getting all of what you feel out in front of you. It may seem like you sense something deep inside, but there is no substitute for looking straight at a quality within your being. If growth is your goal, calmly evaluate your progress on an ongoing basis to open the doorways of higher vibration. No judgment is necessary; awareness is the main ingredient to the alchemical stew. Take note of discrepancies and correct them as you go. Many habits will have to be unlearned, and new conscious acts born to take their place.

If you don't know what you are meant to do, knowing everything you aren't meant to do will bring you much closer to finding out. If there are a hundred paths in front of you, and you can eliminate 90 of them, you can focus more closely on the 10 left over. On each path there are lessons to learn. Some will work more easily and then you will know you are on the right track. Synchronicities will appear, and suddenly the path you are meant to walk will light up under your feet. Each step will bring the joy of discovery and the fulfillment that comes from living truth.

Every moment is an opportunity for undertaking this most noble of quests. Take delight when you learn that you dislike the taste of radishes. You have learned something about yourself! It is a sign of your freedom and uniqueness. A "bad" thing can be every bit as beneficial as a "good" one when seen from meditation. In fact when you remove judgment they become the same – experience. Meditation is outside 'frame of reference'. Everything 'is' and the observer is a part of it. Welcome to the happening that is you. Experiment and enjoy!

Ruminations of the Universe

Enlightenment
Profound Aspects of the Soul

A life lived encounters difficulty and times of trial. In every circumstance there is a lesson. As so many fine friends remind me, there is no failure and no regret. Looking back and second guessing a choice can undermine the strength that you gain when you stand behind a decision. It is precisely in these pressure filled circumstances that we carve out our own unique identity. In one sense, trials are an opportunity to make manifest the deepest and most profound aspects of your soul.

When one feels an influx of Love rushing in for support at a specifically challenging point upon the path, the wind suddenly moves to your back and each step becomes steadier. Prayers give the tendency for things to go well, for adversity to disperse, and for Love to return as the guiding force and upholder of all. Wrapped in a blanket of good tidings the complex becomes simple again. Experience leads to Understanding which becomes Wisdom and awakens Awareness.

It is a blessing to be uncertain about tomorrow. What control does one have over nature's inclination? Rest easy knowing that being yourself is the best you can do. Accruing responsibility where none lies can be worse than doing nothing at all. We need only bring our gifts to the surface and share them with one another. This is the solution to every problem. Wars and wickedness come from blockages; pockets of energy that have been diverted from their natural course. When we heal ourselves and restore this flow, we resonate well-ness which makes it possible for others to pick up the vibe.

Believe in people and they will believe in you. God is in every creature and is looking through their eyes. Give Love and get some in return. Teach this to your friends. Let go of that which is beyond reach. Relax and slow down. Give life a chance to touch your heart and open the grace of spirit. It is in the sunrise and in the rainbow on a misty summer day. It is in the starry night and the call of the owl at dusk. Everywhere you look, the glory of creation is shimmering with brilliance. Keep reminding yourself of what is truly important and live that way.

Much Love and tidings of ever new joy,

Enlightenment
Hurl Yourself Forward to Full Humanity

Winding through the infinite possibilities, all potentials become actual and the hidden becomes known. Treading a path through space we walk with attentiveness and remain centered come what may. There are hills and valleys both figuratively and literally. Rolling along the surface, the beauty of the new supercedes the pettiness of the details. Deep inside we know what to do and that all is one.

Suddenly we find ourselves in the body…NOW! But you say you remember yesterday? Well show it to me…alas it is nowhere to be found. Recover your full alertness to this moment and you will have discontinuity with your reflections on past and congruence with that which actually is. Perhaps ye striveth hard for the 'morrow. Well fellow traveler, this is but a reflection of that which has already come and gone, never to be again.

The moments when you most feel you'd like to escape, hurl yourself forward. There are numerous thresholds of resistance, but none too opaque for the light of the heart to shine through. Cat-like we lurk, relaxed yet ready to spring to life with full force immediately! If you wish to know what it is to be fully human…the true human that is just emerging, it is simply a matter of making it a priority. But I need time for this and that, you might say. 'Tis a pity.

Enlightenment
The Peace of Space

No matter how enthralling the astral realms become to the seeker who suddenly realizes that the 3D world is nothing but the surface of a vast universe of vibration, they must always remember that beyond it all is the Peace of Space. Beyond the Mind world which interprets the senses and acts as an intermediary between your being and existence OUT THERE, there is consciousness. This is something you do not need to strive to maintain. When you get past the concept that there is something more to be had, you can settle into the idea that ALL IS AS IT SHOULD BE, including YOU.

This does not mean that we stop striving to grow in our understanding. A perfect moment can evolve into another perfect moment that has built upon the experience of the past. Future will beckon us to a day when our troubles will go away, until we realize that the horizon never comes any closer. Sinking in to who and how you are now, you start to touch the deeper dimensions. You phase in to the present and realize that all along things were more vibrant and alive than you had ever noticed. You become a part of nature's melody and delight in its song.

So many of us have inclinations in this regards but feel as if it can not work in our reality. Often this is because we have yet to value our own inner voice enough to create what we perceive. Each person's unique ability has to develop over time and learn how it fits into the work of the whole. When seeing yourself from outside of yourself it is easier to recognize your own tendencies and then foster curiosity wherever it might lead. Share your discoveries with friends around the Earth and those that resonate with you will find you.

We are truly moving into the age of the world family. No longer do we need to be bound by small units when people everywhere have gifts to share. Many of our soul selves know each other and have been intermittently connected for aeons. One life is not nearly enough to explore the friendship possibilities. Death may cut short a journey in the body, but it does nothing to interrupt the soul's path. We all come and go many times. While we are here we have the precious opportunity to share the blessings of Life.

Enlightenment
Absurd Universal Secrets

The Universe has many secrets and as Osho used to say, most of them are out in the open. Staring us in the face are the most amazing things, but it is all so immense that we cannot see. Being breathed by that which is…immersed in a sea of bliss….we imagine ourselves to be lonely and separate. Even now I can hear the music of the Lotus Paradise, not as a metaphor but as an eternal celebration. If you are interpreting this….STOP! Be silent and listen. Let the birds and bugs take you to the song of the Earth. Let the sun dance upon your heart and awaken the recognition of your soul. Reflecting like the moon, the mystery is as enjoyable as the music.

George W. this, terrorists that….everybody is Hitler….yeah yeah… What is it for? The hopelessness of the world will eventually frustrate us so bad that we turn in the other direction. At last!!! So that is what the madness is all about. Finally we realize that fulfillment will never be found without. Everybody isn't going to wake up at once. It happens one individual at a time. Shout loud enough and you'll get killed. Help people where they are and with what they can handle and little by little we'll get the Earth back on track. It takes awhile for the greater revelations to sink in to the collective subconscious. Rushing is violence and then Love is replaced with Power that starts seeking its own glory.

Now if you are ready to go all the way to the truth which lies beyond boundary, lean in a little closer. No religion is the answer because they are all filtered through the perception of the original sage that spawned them (not to mention the echoes of their friends and friends of friends throughout time). It is better to say to Jesus, Buddha, Lao Tzu, and the rest of the gang, "Thank you for your creative expression. Now let's see what mine will be." Let's freshen things up. Blow away the dust and seriousness of the tired old stories. Church bores people because it is like watching the same movie a thousand times. No matter how entertaining it is, eventually it will make you want to slit your wrist.

Life is ever new and always changing. You can't get a fix on it and it often throws you the absurd. Whisper hello to the giraffe and maybe he'll tell you from where he gets his spots. Why do beloveds sometimes get taken away from us in the prime of their lives? To shock us and remind us to get with Life while we have this short and fleeting chance to dance the dance. Forget all this bullshit war business. Those who kill (regardless of their reason) will have marks upon their head. Laugh and dance and never let those status quo bastards take away your joy. Make some noise in public and when they scowl say, "Yes I am a little strange, nice to meet you stiffy."

Ruminations of the Universe

Enlightenment
Did We Die and Come Here?

Most religions define the afterlife as a place where we are free of some of the burdens of Earth and where more of what we hope for out of existence is easily attainable. Another way to look at this proposition is that what occurs after this world is seemingly more desirable than what happens in this world. It doesn't take long to see the reverse of what we normally think and ask the question, "Did we die and come here?" Perhaps the punishment we fear is the one we are living and giving to ourselves. Maybe we don't like to talk about death because it will inevitably lead us to realize that we are already dead and this is what we hide from most of all. Losing track of our soul being and its greater continuity we suffer the trauma of compression and the interference of the magnificent zombie well wishers.

True life does not manifest through human form until originality springs from the fountain. Habits and training do not make a holy human. The ability to bring the new and become a vessel for grace in the world is a reflection of godly force. Forget concepts, God is Life. They are not separate. The only father in the sky is the sun, and yes He does have a consciousness, and yes you can interact with your father's thoughts. Ra,

Apollo, Helios, or Uncle Charlie….whatever you call him, you will only hear an answer when you can meet him and speak his language. When you see the illuminati use his symbol, you will know that the truth is being subverted. Thou shall not worship the image of the father, but the father himself. Fear is indicative of the False One, the shadow.

The astral realms are preparing for the influx of many souls. There are simply too many people for what has been socially achieved. If the technological solutions were applied, ocean habitats cultivated, and space travel pursued with focus and determination, more numbers would not be an issue. It would actually be desirable when considering space colonization, starting with the Moon, Mars, Saturn's Moons, and one day Venus. Anything we can stand on, we will eventually do so. As humanity has climbed Everest, so too will spirit move civilization to realize most of its innate potential in time. There are secret organizations that are already well on the way to some of these things out of sight of the people.

If only more of you would give up the mundane for the surreal, then the artistic attitude would lift some of the menace that faces us in the marketplace. There is a chill in the air, that a little warmth of awakening could help lift. Don't look to report your neighbor, when they have not harmed you in any way. Being a servant of spies you will cause karma by breaking human decency and be bound to the result. Denial will only get facists so far. When they self-destruct we step out of the way. When bombs fly, we duck. When empty rhetoric spews onto the airwaves, we deconstruct. When the thought police knocks on our mind, we smile and thank God that we have control and can simply watch everything. One day we will drop the body and it will come to each of us very soon. 5 years or 50, it all goes by in a blip. There is no time to waste doing things we don't love. You can choose to wait, but that will just make it a bit tougher when circumstances come down on illusions.

Ruminations of the Universe

Enlightenment
Still Naked in the Garden

The shattering understanding that occurs with the openness of meditation is something that is still very new to western minds. For some reason the mystical has been condemned. It is an echo of the belief's held by the puritanical settlers that first bumbled their way upon New England's shores. "Witchcraft! Heresy! Something to be feared!" they shouted. Nothing could be further from the truth. This is the harmful byproduct of the Christian indoctrination that many still subject themselves to every Sunday. It excludes much from the potential experience of the adherent. Many become uptight and out of touch with heart or soul. Bound by rules, morality, and judgment they build up tension and then wonder why they later break down. It also surprises them when people start fleeing their 'Jesus Saves!' mentality.

The strange thing about it is, that this Jesus fellow, whoever he happened to be, was most likely very tuned into the mystical. He spoke the language of the day to the people around him. Of course it is good to remember that the stories we hear from him weren't written down until long after the events supposedly transpired. Tales of sages regularly get mixed up with older legends from other traditions. Blown up and dramatized, they become archetypal representations of aspects of the human condition. Discovering an individual link to the Universe, the flow of Life suddenly makes clear what the search was all about. Jesus directly perceived the same thing the Yogis of the East describe and something any being can become aware of and know first hand. Sink in a little deeper and you will see that all you thought was solid was simply the surface.

Jesus was taught about Past Lives, Chakras and Auras. His light emanated to all of those around him. 'Drink of me,' he said and you can absorb his energy even to this day. The masters never disappear. Bask in the glow of one who is enlightened. Unified with Source they speak as Existence itself. This is the secret of the Oracle at Delphi. The body becomes a vehicle for transmitting truth vibrations. It is a great evolutionary success that can be juxtaposed with the despair of many souls lost along the way. Consciousness is a very sacred gift. Strip away that which is superimposed. Layers and layers of identification have to be highlighted and released. It is the most amazing experience to see the world with clean eyes; to be brand new underneath the sun actually feeling the moment.

Enlightenment

What a joy to be able to tell someone unashamedly that you love them and that you wish for peace so that others might share in what you have come to cherish.

The Earth is singing a beautiful song. If you listen closely you see that all of nature is a symphony. Every day is a miracle. People only doubt God's existence because they cannot see the obvious. Constantly referencing acquired knowledge they conclude that they know what is going on and miss the wonder of the now. Familiarization with an object causes it to lose its luster for them. One who practices mindfulness rarely gets brought into such dullness. Reflecting life as it is free of interpretations and the logging away of events in the storehouse of the mind, they have bright eyes which display a good natured sense of humor. It is really very funny when you see the reality of our situation. We paint so many elaborate pictures and involve each other in such serious situations but really we are still naked in the garden.

Ruminations of the Universe

Enlightenment
Mind Liberation

Take a moment to slow down and pay attention to what is to follow. This is particularly so if you have realized that the mind mechanism that grinds the gears of past and invokes fears for the future is not a reality in itself, but simply a communication tool that has turned on its master. The greatest enemies of humanity are those that take this gift of a beautiful information processing instrument and use it to harm the owner who was never allowed to know how to use it properly. The Mind is a topic to be discussed thoroughly and exhaustively, for only when you know every cranny and/or nook, will you be able to relax the tension that invades your brain.

You believe that you have a good reason to stew in your own juices, but this is just how the Mind continues to deceive. Looking at it one way, there are 3 kinds of people in the world right now: those who are free of their mind, those who are under control, and those who are on the fence. Those who are on the fence are in the worst position because they will be in constant anguish. Essentially it is unsustainable to live in both worlds. If you start to wake up and try to continue diving into the old world, you are masochistic to be sure. It is much better to move forward and go on with things. No doubt, it is utterly terrifying. Being lost and lonely is worse.

One more time just for fun: You have 5 senses and they make an imprint in the mind. This Mind is not you. It is just the conglomerated image produced by the moment to moment synthesis of the slice of reality that each sense perceives. These are the windows which the soul can use to look out. If not occupied with awareness, they are susceptible to infiltration which leaves you open to manipulation. If you want real security you better learn about all the ways people are trying to send data through your senses and into your Mind. Any way you define yourself through the filters of the outer world you are reducing your cosmic self.

You can literally feel all the stars in the sky as your cosmic body and all the thoughts of the universe at once as your cosmic mind. Aum vibration unifies all things and is like a great cosmic graph underlying Creation. There is a chain of manifestation reaching from 6D down to 3D. It spirals like a fractal or a tree branch reaching towards subtlety. There is much momentum in the forward expression so it is a wonder that we can dive back upstream like

Enlightenment

salmon searching for the Source. Only those with a great yearning for truth will make it to the end of the journey. It is a surprise to find that the end is when you realize there is no end.

Blast out those foreign thought troops from your noodle. Build a front at your aura's edge. Then you can run constant security checks on all unsecured information. When love or sex arises you may let down your guard and enjoy. Sharing creatively you can build your own world instead of letting reality be dictated to you. Just knowing this great trick will allow you much space and freedom. It is all a grand play. Sometimes you can perform as the hero and sometimes the villain. Other times you can simply be the fly on the wall. All of these perspectives are processed by the Universe. When you become one with Universe you can see/be all roles ever played past, present or future.

Ruminations of the Universe

Enlightenment
Roam Free in the Wilderness

When you find it in your heart to follow the Tao, you will live a different life than those who make their way based on the laws of the world. Your peaks and valleys will be much more intense. This will help develop an absolutely level consciousness which can watch everything and remain aware. Others who find solace in routine and security will slowly become numb and the shining heart will become cloaked in darkness. The finest subtleties of the synapses become dull and the mind rationalizes clinging to the same old same old. Only a lion with the strength to let forth a full roar will be able to again and again shake the shackles and roam free in the wilderness.

Friends and foes alike may doubt your steps. How can another know what the Tao whispers in your ear? There is no validation necessary to walk in the present going where the inclination leads you. Knowing that the universe will provide you with what you need, the fear subsides and there is clarity. Human feelings are felt in all their depth. You will experience the journey and watch it. You are Human and God. Somewhere underneath it all is order. Anything the human mind can come up with is but a subset of the universal order – Tao. If you align with the universal order all other form will be at your disposal. This is why many artists and musicians become meditators.

All the images that are flashed before us every day shape our perceptions in ways that are thoroughly unhealthy. We are filled with expectations and rigid conceptions of reality. We are persuaded to feel as if we are always lacking. Very few live the full set of societal ideals and if we were to speak with those who do would we find them any happier than anybody else? Perhaps they might even feel worse having found that success in the world has still left them empty in spirit. We must see this discrepancy between the worldly way that we are always told about and the spiritual way which is rarely discussed. There are more profound laws than the ones in your books.

It is time to trust yourself over those who might advise you. There are most likely many others pulling you down, but a million reasons to do nothing about it. If you think it might be scary and difficult, you are quite correct. There is nothing about life on Earth that is easy but true Love. That is something we all seek underneath the surface. To find someone who understands us and will hold our hand with a reverence for our sacred nature. To attract such a Love we must be ready to accept it when it comes. Do we find ourselves worthy of a Love that will change our lives? You might be surprised how some people protect their misery. It is just another thing to distract from the real.

To trust so deeply that even if the Universe leads you off a cliff you will jump is to have complete surrender. Was this not the state of Christ on the Cross? He could have escaped but His heart must have told Him that to die was to live. Life is what you create. Watch closely what you resonate because that is what you are drawing to you. Remember also that nobody is perfect. Universal laws are not something to use in order to judge yourself. Keep trying your best to align and give yourself some time and room to breath. Being forgiving to yourself, you can forgive others and set everyone free.

Ruminations of the Universe

Enlightenment
The Most Spectacular Gift in Existence

There are many forces at work out there my friends. We are not and could never be an island unto ourselves. We will bump into friends, foes, and lovers no matter how dizzy our wanderings. Within each of our human associates the divine spark and precious qualities of eternity are just waiting to be nurtured.

Some say God works in mysterious ways. I am reminded of the masquerade balls during the European enlightenment of the late 1700's and early 1800's. Potential lovers playing hide and seek with each other. The thrill of the unknown hanging in the air... Are we not all dressed in costumes playing like this? In the East it is called Leela, the cosmic game.

The twinkle in every eye has a heavenly source. Our whole universe is thriving with life. There is a heartbeat that underlies all of creation. The same spirit that breathes you pulses the stars and sends galaxies spiraling through space. How can there be separation when vibration is everywhere? Aum has a few special secrets to tell you. Deep within the present all things will be revealed.

What a joy it is to open the heart! Many people read trivia and think they are getting a handle on what is happening here. Release the desire to hold on and your experience will take a new luster of brilliance. Don't be shy; shout your truth to the sky. Whisper it to the wind. Share a tune with the Earth and your sublime realizations with the Sun. Lose your mind and you'll feel fine.

Slow down and find gratitude for what you have. It is a miracle to be here and be alive. We can dream about winning the lottery, but we already have something much rarer and worth infinitely more. Throw your diamonds into the river and discover where real value lies. With the most spectacular gift in existence already our own, there is no need to scrounge like beggars.

My friends, you are so much more than this. Believe yourself worthy and you will laugh when you awaken to that which has been the case all along.

Enlightenment
Transcendent Glory is Everywhere

No matter how down you might feel, wait just a little longer and the pendulum will start swinging back up. If you are riding high, maintain some space, because just as certainly things will ebb once more. This is why Buddha's non-attachment is such a wise and valuable practice. Life may go up and down, but we can remain centered. As Osho said just before he left the body behind, "You are a witness."

Consciousness does not think, it reflects. There is no better way to sort through the complexities of being human. We have thoughts, feelings, and intuition. How can we hear the voice of our own soul if we are constantly occupied with values imposed by the outside and unresolved pain from our own past? It takes a little time to find the knack of disconnection from impulse. We go back to Buddha's bag of tricks to find the practice of non-doing.

Often people truly believe they are their thoughts, so they move with every little inclination. Next time you feel compelled to react, stop and wait. Where did this message to act come from? Do you really want to give so much control away to your environment? There should be no buttons to push. Buddha says if someone disturbs you,

you should thank them for showing you a part of yourself that you have yet to come to know. Serenity arises when you can rest in yourself and glide through the world untouched.

We also have to recover the lost parts of ourselves that are still frozen in space. All the times when we were unable to fully express the truth of who we are we left a bit of ourselves behind. This unresolved pain works behind the scenes and is very often the source of why we might react so vociferously to generally harmless stimuli. There is much fear for people to go in search of these stranded pieces because they try to avoid the pain and suffering initially felt when these parts were lost. What they don't realize is that they will always feel it until this is faced.

It is up to heart and its tears to reinvigorate our fragments and welcome them back into the whole with unconditional love. After this discrepancy is bridged the energy that used to move in a destructive manner will begin to serve creation. The holy spirit of creativity will move us and we will live our life purpose. As the creator of our world we merge with the great creator and are no longer separate. The whole universe rejoices at our homecoming and we realize the transcendent glory that is everywhere just below the surface.

Enlightenment
It is Something Else You Seek

The rebelliousness that arises from the inner call of independence serves to create space in which to observe natural tendencies. Escaping from one trap, it is important not to fall into another. Anything that becomes a habit or a catch-all response to similar stimuli forms a new mental barrier in place of the old one. A human who is truly free does not need to assert it.

There is the impetus from personal will and that which is the reflection of inner blossoming. With the first, you change your own course and struggle; with the second, you are moved by the river of life to a most blessed destination. Energized by right action, good perpetuates good.

Many times people work against the very things they wish to attain. Give what you love value and it will become a bigger part of your life. Only the individual knows the whispers of their own heart. Often they already know why they are unhappy but feel powerless to change the direction. Find where the heart is and live according to it. Then it is God's will that you manifest.

Too often we carry the burden of perceived judgment which keeps us from expressing completely. Short circuited at the outset, the flow never gets an opportunity to create new synapse tributaries. Again and again the old thought patterns justify themselves into existence. Dear traveler, it is something else you seek.

You can be for something or against it and still you will be bound. See and be. Awareness observes all and has limitless possibilities at its command. Illuminating every option at once, there is no need to choose. In tune with the moment, without doubt, you will find the way.

Enlightenment
Open the Door and Ye Shall See

Hey, did you hear the latest news? Something happened here…and something happened there. Someone died, someone lived. Smatterings of tragedy and those small but significant stories where someone does something we can all feel good about. Jimmy hits a home run that beats the rival. Sally won the spelling contest. Little Egbert made a crazy looking gadget and won 2nd place at the science fair.

Where does the meaning come from that we give our lives? Comparing your own path to others will always bring confusion. Keep on your own road for your own lessons. They all end up going where they need too. Temptations can indeed lead you astray. They are many and the benefits to the spiritual path are extremely arduous to attain. You walk alone in the night and shake the foundations of this world.

Take your daily dose and don't feel too bad about it. John Lennon and Elton John sang, "Whatever gets you through the night…is alright…alright." There is some real truth to that. A friend recently reminded me that if I survived the day then I did something. You give it a shot and let it roll. Remember to make time to do something creative. Take a walk or a bike ride through a neighborhood.

There is a random element to the Universe that we all should be grateful for. Even if we are not worthy and even if we have made a million mistakes, we can still find love. The Earth blooms through her creatures and we give our hearts. The song is sung; the celebration is at long last joined! Alleluia, praise God! Yes. There is such a thing as holiness in a totally non-preconceived sort of way. Open the door and ye shall see.

Enlightenment
Symphony of Life

Wow, I'm still here. Literally I am amazed. This hunk of flesh keeps hurling forward through space. I am barely connected to the body yet I look out of these eyes. Here and there, seeing many levels of existence at once, every atom of the soul perceives a billion subtleties. Communing with the cosmos and talking with a friend, the way forward is a bit at a time. Standing on a planet with my head in the stars, I can hear many songs at night. You and I are each one of the universe's melodies. No matter what you do you will be in the Symphony of Life.

Let us get to the bottom of the search. An interest in metaphysics is compelled by a yearning to know what one intuitively feels are the true mysteries. Life cannot be about a 9 to 5'er and a microcosm of personal dramas. We can play that role for awhile but eventually we will all tire of the game. There is something greater calling to all of us. Each one who realizes makes it a little easier for the next. Creating a climate of wisdom, flowers start blooming. A garden of enlightenment becomes the joy of the Earth. Darkness is dispersed naturally.

Follow your intuition when it comes to politics. A

slick campaign can make your skin crawl. Who seems to be sincere? Who seems to work for the same forces keeping the populace in fear? If there are none you resonate with, create an alternative. Form an opinion and give it a try. The secret is to be total in your action. We need a transcendent system that works in accord with universal law to the benefit of all. There should be plenty of time to enjoy the beaches of the Earth and travel. Water must be cleaned throughout the world. There is no excuse for the extinction of species.

One day 3000 years from now if someone is still here, they may believe the stories of great beasts that roamed the Earth to be myths that were never real. After all, the beauty of a tiger is pretty farfetched. Not to mention the absurd wonder of the giraffe and sensitive magnitude of the elephant. When they are gone, who will be there to remind humanity? A time capsule with photos is not the same as a relationship with a living creature. We all loved the Croc Hunter because he gave voice to the animals. He remembered himself as an animal.

Outside the city walls nature awaits us. Relax the mind and allow the imagination to fill in the astral world just outside of our own. No more doubts stopping up the psychic process. Trust in

Enlightenment

yourself and follow your own path. Each moment will build upon the next and the seeds you sew will bring an abundant harvest. There is always time to make a change as long as you are alive. When you move on to the astral realm there will be other adventures, but before long you will be on the next trip here to do it all over again. There is no escaping destiny, so it is best to enjoy it.

Ruminations of the Universe

Enlightenment
Word from Home Planet

Bloggers, you are loved and never more than when you stick it to the man. Fearlessly proclaiming haphazard truths willy nilly all silly in the wind... That is reality now. Data streams with happy camper smiles taking time just to opine. Anything goes out here in space; while we race to that line we chase. See through all the lies and what does it get you? Perhaps a good article; perhaps you will have opened someone's eyes. Then what are they going to do and are you at all responsible?

A little essay shouldn't scare anyone. A few words here and there deliberately misplaced. A mind can unwind and find something sublime. There never were any rules…. Imitations are limitations and something you should do once just to get the taste of and then be finished! Do what strikes your fancy. When someone is shocked, tell them not to worry, this is what someone who is alive looks like. If they get pissed, dance away and sing carols in their memory.

Stop and think to yourself 10 times, "Jesus, Buddha, and Krishna are figments of my imagination." Scary thought? No guilt, no shame. Even if those dudes were real, they would allow you that much freedom would they not? What makes the pages of one book surreal and another dismal? Is it magic? Is it tragic when several men are lost for a cause that someone else forgot? It is time for all despair to gain clarity and disappear in the air. Only then will relief and release be possible; peace is possible.

Out of the pen and munchin' the grave, free range spirits catch heights that the weighed down have never found. You will feel sorrow, but go ahead and fly away. They won't find you where you are going. Be thankful that the Earth is such a noble gal. She could never let her foolish kids kill her. Sun will burn everybody before that ever happens anyway. That is the true cause of your weather catastrophes: disharmony amongst each other and lack of union between your designs and the nature of your home planet.

Super Channeling

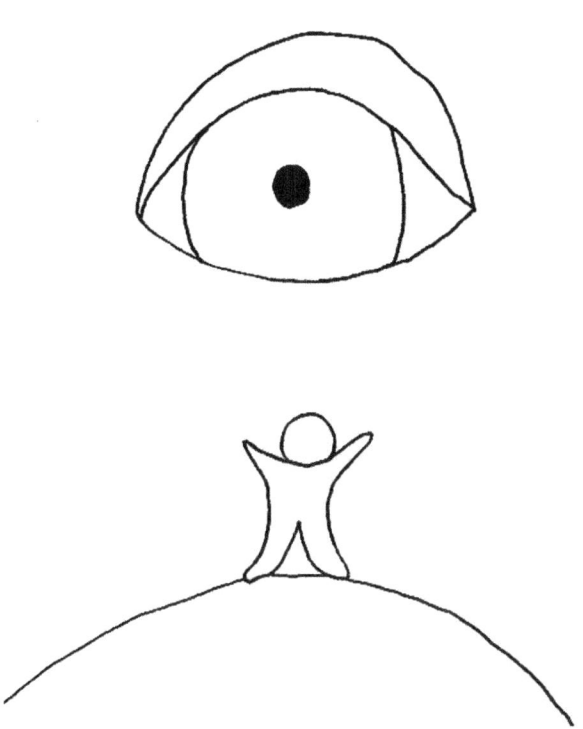

Super Channeling
Coming Down to Earth

After aeons of traveling through space, it isn't always easy to pack the whole of what you are into a tiny little Earth vessel. Many spiritually advanced souls have difficulties traversing the idiosyncrasies of physical creation because they long to be immersed solely in the freedom of consciousness. The complications of the body and the world do not seem to apply to the heart and the pulsing lotus blossom existence. Somewhere deep within every circumstance is a lesson to extract and assimilate. Misery flees when understanding illuminates awareness in the moment.

Considering the chakras, an old soul can be born with a well-developed heart center and an open third eye. They still have to go through what everyone else does, so often their lower chakras will be messed up with brainwashing, emotional trauma, and sexual misunderstanding. The sensitive spirit will suffer even more than the burgeoning soul because they will feel the pain more poignantly and in many cases there is no one there to explain what is happening. They will then want to disconnect and live only in dreamland instead of here and there simultaneously.

Ruminations of the Universe

The anguish of the artist/musician/philosopher can be explained in this manner. Aware of and connected to the beautiful things in life amidst a crowd that seems hostile and violent, they feel isolated. Throughout Western Art there is a thorough mixing of beauty and pain. Some even think the pain is necessary to fuel the fires of creation, but it is not so. Creation comes spontaneously from the Joy of being alive and cognizance of the gift of life. Naturally as part of the universe we have our own song to express.

Deprogramming the mind, healing the emotions and cultivating a healthy attitude toward sex will make more room in the vessel for the spirit to come down. Then rather than hovering around the body, it will shine through it. Bad habits will cease and demons will lose their ability to influence because there is no open space in the body to jump into. If the soul is vacant, possession will happen. It is really a quite frequent occurrence. Luckily in most cases it is only for a fleeting sensation, but one should beware because if they allow it, the demon will make your home theirs.

With the help of spirit guides, ancestors, angels, and our own higher self, we can transform the blockages and establish a freely flowing connection to the universal source. Demons, though prevalent are generally very impotent little creatures. They lurk in the shadows and if there are none, they are nowhere to be found. We are very powerful divine beings that have come here to experience the wonders of Earth in a human body. No context can contain us. Let it all go and you will be free. Happiness comes as a byproduct of removing limitation.

Ruminations of the Universe

Super Channeling
Earth and the Galactic Tug of War

Earth is a crossing point for many galactic species. Some souls begin their journey here under the Mother's Love and protection. Many others travel here from other star systems to incarnate and experience the advanced spiritual training derived from living in the 3rd dimension. The student is successful when they can be in the material body and simultaneously experience the 4th dimensional astral realm and the state of awareness that can lift out of even this. Pure consciousness is beyond all manifestation.

Earth is not the first place in this solar system to cultivate the growth of its inhabitants. Before it was destroyed, the asteroid planet (which I like to call Minerva) was a hub of activity. Mars was the first of the 3 inner red planets to host civilization. As the orbit eased ever outward the planet slowly dried up; Martian DNA was sent to Earth. In like manner, the Earth will dry and as Venus moves toward equilibrium it will receive the DNA of humanity. Like seeds it will rain from the sky.

Earth herself pours Love from the 4th dimension into the 3rd. She plays with the Sun and their union imbues the terrestrials with their remarkable tenacity and intelligence. Many of the solar system's other planets have beings around them in other dimensions. Life is not how most of humanity defines it. It is literally everywhere; vibration is the key which unlocks the infinite potential in every atom of existence. Jupiter and Saturn thrive with etheric beings. Mini systems in and of themselves, they follow the Sun's creative lead and manifest worlds of their own. Neptune has air elementals and millions of glowing astral plankton. Uranus is surrounded by a chorus of gentle elder spirits.

Earth is surrounded by many types of aliens. The most familiar to us are the greys said to be from Zeta Reticuli. These scientists often work for the reptilians but secretly maintain a level of independence. They are indeed cross breeding with humans to add soul and depth to their experiencing capacities. Genetic tinkering has weakened this species and rendered them dependent on both the reptilians and the humans for continued survival. We humans must win them over with heart and form a friendship that subverts the reptilian's nefarious tendencies.

Earth also includes beings from Pleiades amongst her brightest stars. Artistic and musical spirits that vibrate on a very high frequency, they often have difficulty being stuck in the human body until they become aware of who they truly are.

After recovering the memory coded directly into their DNA, they are then able to communicate telepathically with the home world. Sending powerful vibes of creativity and love, they help to keep humanity on a spiritual path and avoid the baser desires which so often lead people to ruin.

Earth, like Minerva before her, finds herself strained to the point of breaking with so many forces pulling her in different directions. The weather changes and catastrophes are a direct result of the inharmonious tendencies currently at play on her surface and in the subtle realms all around her. It is only Love for her precious children and the focus of the Sun's creative vision assisted by Sirian seers and ancient masters scattered across our own globe that keep it all together.

Earth's destiny is not preordained. All of the characters involved have free will and so can enact any number of scenarios. It is up to each of us to dig for the deeper truth and then live these spiritual ideals every day. When we add our creative energies to nature's choir of goodness, the darkness disappears from our hearts and therefore has one less foothold in the world. In this cosmic tug of war there is struggle and there is joy. Whatever happens to the physical, each of us has the opportunity to find individual salvation. Here or there, love will set us free.

Super Channeling
Angels Among Us

Even now around you are angels. A rainbow of colors and a myriad of personalities, this type of being is as much of a reality as any human. There are some that have actually entered human bodies to help anchor the spiritual energies, and some that work from the astral, generally assisting the endeavors of those on the ground. Together they are building a seamless bridge between the 3rd and 4th dimension.

Beyond the 4th dimensional main body of angels, are the archangels. They represent Unity beyond time/space events. They can jump in anywhere on the timeline and send energy to balance situations. They are not bound by an adherence to "ask and ye shall receive" as are most angels. Their responsibilities rise beyond this and their position has been earned by aeons of life experience.

An average person can act as a conduit for the angels when a specific incidence arises. Like a cosmic switchboard, angels can activate or influence those receptive to spiritual energies. It is all a part of the intricate web of synchronicities that form around steady intent. Patience is necessary and will be rewarded. Failure is not possible on a heartfelt mission. Sincere vibrations bring about a positive result.

In every room with people, angels are there.

Together we share.

Super Channeling
Archangels and Spirit Warriors

Harmonizing the chakras so that the aura glows true, the spirit warriors of Earth proceed to the next stages of human evolution. Unable to grasp even the simplest of spiritual ideas, the old model of human will fade into non-existence within the next hundred or so years. Even as we no longer see Neanderthal, we shall no longer see the Homo Sapiens. We have heard rumors about Homo Novus, and these rumors carry the seeds of a new beginning. This human is not angry or dominating…couldn't be. These are behaviors shed with the limitations of belief and body obsession. The vibrations of the community will be too high to leave any wound unhealed.

Having awakened the heart, the New Human clearly sees in the physical and the astral realm. The 5 senses and mental duality are fully understood and incorporated into the basic parameters of the embodying circumstance. Energy systems will be taught in schools even as mathematics and reading are today. It is your very being and potential. Those who cling to the rigidity of yesteryear will suffer much unnecessarily. There is no way back to the days of ignorance and localized exclusion. Thank God for it! The responsibility is returned back to every individual to find for themselves a way to incorporate universal awareness into near body perspective.

Every time a human experiences new spiritual territory, they open it up as a possibility for others. We can bring the new into our reality through being creative. In this way we participate in Creation and have an effect on each other's growth. With the hierarchy of beings assisting us in this exploration of love and freedom, we sing out mighty and glorious alleluias in exaltation to the most high - Source. Dancing with the intricate subtleties of this Aum vibration we come to know that things were never meant to be so serious. All the hardship was to bring you back to the celebration. It is and always was something other than what you thought; this discovery brings release.

A good friend Archangel Gabriel has visited me both in the flesh and through the channeling of his higher self through another willing facilitator. Gabriel is opening up space throughout the galaxy. Looking over musicians, artists, and writers, He fosters inspiration and has long worked side by side with the beings who are his brothers and sisters in spirit. Playing his heart trumpet, He gives courage to those committed to protecting the eternal flame of truth. Gabriel loves to observe the drop falling from the leaf into the pond of stillness. Your soul family goes on and on.

Ruminations of the Universe

Super Channeling
Angels Come From Pleiadies

Long before coming to grace the Earth with their benign presence, many angels existed in their full cosmic glory in the higher dimensional realm located in the area of space we look towards when marveling at the star cluster Pleiadies – the 7 sisters. Many still reside there as it is one of their homes and one of the few places they can actually be born into existence. From this location they are living extensions of cosmic mind and still have full cognizance of the unity of their heartbeat and the heartbeat of the absolute. Born into awareness, they soak in the energy of the universe until they are drawn to a star system that needs their unique healing talents, patience and virtue.

For those angels that have come to Earth, even remaining in the astral realms constituted by the planet's aura and the projections of her children is an arduous journey which calls for relentless self-sacrifice. Following humanity's progress since its inception, they are our immediate spiritual caretakers. Often they influence events to have a tendency to work out better than they might have otherwise. From avoiding accidents, to helping you find a parking spot in a busy city, they are very involved in the intimate day to day occurrences of life.

Some have even taken it upon themselves to enter into human bodies so as to have a more hands on approach to human development. Many of our master teachers were angels incarnate. After going through the densification process to enter this sphere, even angels can become forgetful of who they truly are. Often it takes another angel who has remembered their true self to help awaken another. Much lucidity is needed for this extensive downloading of information.

There are also some beings among you who used to be of high spiritual vibrations in the celestial arenas that are now using their Earthly power in a malevolent way. These fallen angels could rise again if only they would recover their connection to the universal pulse. Mistaking themselves as separate and beyond restriction, they have a blind spot in their reckoning that will ultimately lead to their demise. The good news is that life gives many opportunities for all of us to get it right.

Some of you reading this might have Pleiadian angelic heritage. Whisper to yourself, "I am Pleiadian," and see how it feels. You have been in Atlantis, Egypt, Greece, Rome, North America, and every major civilization. Some of you have been benevolent and some have run amok. Some have played the game of being a leader and others have gently assisted humanity from behind the scenes. Even while in the body you can recover your astral wings. Then when you drop the body, you can fly anywhere in the universe.

Ruminations of the Universe

Super Channeling
Healing Patterns of Angels

One way angels can reach people is through succinct aphorisms communicated through intuition. An example is a time I was sent the message, "You do not have to prove yourself, be yourself." Another active way they can get involved with healing and repair is through their actual flight pattern. They might start doing circular laps over your head to assist in loosening up mental resistance. To restore connection in a relationship they may adopt a larger scale flight pattern such as the infinity symbol.

In this manner they are able to directly align the energy of our auras. When the active healing is finished, they might withdraw to a higher and larger circular pattern with occasional diagonal crisscrossing in the middle. This is how several angels can get involved with your soul evolution. The intuitive message is usually the work of one, your closest and as some say personal guardian angel. If you can perceive flight patterns going on around you, you can be certain that a significant happening is taking place.

Ruminations of the Universe

Super Channeling
Ra, Rainbows, and Freedom from the Body

How does one go about cracking the psychic hold that causes most people to think that the reality they live in is entirely defined by the body and senses? No wonder there is such misery! Almost all of humanity falsely believes ideologies that cause them to be literally imprisoned…chained to a container of dirt and water. Can you put the sky in a jar? Can you put a cloud in a box? Can you put the ocean in a glass? The question then moves to how to provoke a response that tricks one out of the parameters they usually interpret everything with. Here goes something…

Start with utter silence, stillness, and emptiness. All of a sudden something stirs (Intent) and sends out vibrations into space. These vibrations then become more organized as the 'One who intends' starts to become aware. The vibrations coalesce into patterns with their own unique integrity. The being that results is in unity with the "One who intends" and "One on its Own". This 'One on its Own' replicates the process and creates another level of entity…and so on and so on…

Around the very dense manifestation of our physical body, is a light body. This consists of 7 major chakras divided into a typical rainbow of colors and an aura that makes an oval around the body. This is a fact that should be shared with all who do not know it yet. There is no speculation or religiousness involved with it. It is so. If there is a rainbow, one can logically assume that there is a singular white light behind it which gets split somehow. The prism is Ra, the entity in the Sun Body. The split occurs as AUM passes through.

Your senses have been designed to meet the world on the outside. This is the skin of Life….just a surface coating. Many insist on looking outward for fulfillment. A whole culture has been built up based on this false assumption. Humanity creates traps for each other and seems to delight in suffering. The art of separation from sensations is an all but lost one in the modern world. Those who maintain this knowledge are keepers of the flame much as there have been in other epochs of Earthly civilization where insanity seemed to reign supreme.

There are no countries, and there are no religions. Sure some talk about such things, but I can't see them anywhere. I can feel life and see how nature somehow keeps flowing and growing in spite of all human concerns. We may sometimes have to pay a heavy price for being here, but usually only when we stray far from the Tao. If you let your Mind make your decisions for you, you will have a Heart that longs to be integrated. If you draw conclusions, plotting and planning, how can God give you a gift that is unknown?

Angels, demons, aliens, and gods are out there somewhere, yet we go beyond. The Soul is directly connected to Source from which all things come. The characters in the play are only pertinent as long as you are part of the game. When you remember setting the stage in the first place, you can watch both good and bad with a certain amusement. Deaths are impossible unless Karma is involved. Each has a lesson to learn with exactly the right circumstance meeting them at exactly the right time. Even evil can give you many blessings when you turn experience to your advantage.

Process, release, and keep going.

Ruminations of the Universe

Super Channeling
Chakras, Dimensions, and Heavenly Bodies

There is a correlation between chakras, dimensions, and heavenly bodies. Our body/mind is in the 3rd dimension physical reality, our Mother the Earth and Her aura the astral plane extends through the 4th dimension, our Father the Sun is One and our Creative Source in the 5th dimension and Christ Consciousness frees us from all boundaries so we disperse into every atom of Existence in the 6th dimension.

The 3rd chakra rules the body/mind complex and is the highest functioning chakra for many incarnate beings. Working down, the 2nd chakra just above the navel opens the door to the emotions and desires. Beneath this is the root chakra connecting us to our instinctual nature including flight/fight and sex. For many this is the whole of their perspective. They focus on their local environment and live simple lives.

Many humans are evolving from the 3rd dimension to the 4th right now. This is the signature of the Aquarian age and the destination for 2012. We reach this vibration frequency when we open our heart, the 4th chakra. Then we can connect with the Holy Spirit of our Mother Gaia, and express her Will in the world. We sing her song and feel fulfilled in living our purpose. The vision of the garden is returned.

Our 5th chakra is the governor of manifestation. From here we become one with our Father the Sun by becoming Creators in our own right. We give up the personal for the profound and unite with the Source by serving universal truth. In art, speech, and the written word we express as a conduit of the 5th dimensional cosmic mind. In the 4th dimension lies the myth behind that which is born in the 3rd. The 5th contains all myths at once.

We reincarnate as we orbit the Earth in the 4th dimension. We dive down into the 3rd, give up our body and return to the 4th. We then dive down again and again, until we remember the full continuity of our being. Recovering all experience from all lives and piercing the veil of illusion, we begin to build momentum to escape the dense gravity of the Earth. We are done here when we can lift out of the 4th dimension and all that goes with it.

This is only possible with the help of the Sun. There is a process of reincarnating around the Earth, but to even enter the Solar System we needed a light body. Sol (the Sun) gave us each a

Soul and allowed us passageway into the Solar System. The Soul starts out in the 5th dimension and then dives down into the 4th dimensional astral planes of the Earth. Then down into the 3rd dimension existence as a body on the surface of the planet.

Previously beings were allowed to undertake the process of embodiment to experience the planet Minerva (asteroid planet), and also Mars. It is in the plan for the future to have beings take bodies which will work with Venus. One can enjoy the outer planets without taking a body. That is why they fill us with so much awe and inspiration. They remind us of our Soul and the light feeling of freedom we had when we last sailed by them.

With Sol's help we can go back through the portal which brought us into this solar system. It is not easy because we have to leave the Soul behind to get back out. For those who seek to go beyond this point, they will open their third eye 6th chakra and witness the universal secrets first hand. Able to perceive beyond any and all limitation you merge with life itself and are suddenly everywhere. All stars and planets live in you, the Christ Consciousness.

Ruminations of the Universe

Super Channeling
Past Lives: All You Ever Were is Now

When you live in a plastic bubble, your own rationality for what you believe makes sense to you. Therein lies the most dangerous of traps. The more beliefs that enter the bubble, the less light, uniqueness, and soul quality will be able to find its way out. Like black spots on glass, the false assumptions/conclusions add up over time until the only way to have an uncorrupted thought would be to have a life threatening circumstance occur. This kind of happening hacks at fundamental misconceptions which are precisely where anyone who wants to live an independent life has to go. This is why someone who has a near death experience sometimes comes back glowing and vibrant…seemingly a different person. This is why when a few sensitive souls lose a loved one, instead of endless grieving they come back with a deeper sense of spirit and renewed purpose moving forward, honoring their friend by incorporating them into their being.

Most are unable to recall their own past lives due to the compression of internalized expectations. Listening to anyone and everyone as they give you advice and their thoughts about life, you get a confused and simple minded working theory that you then start believing in to give you cover from the fear of death. The fear never goes away and you develop a myriad of behaviors to deal with the increasingly complex outer world. Many of these behaviors become habituated and soon the spark of life begins to die. "Yes sir, no sir, of course I will sacrifice my human dignity…" Plodding along in a daze, drugs and alcohol fill the void and the instigators at the top of the food chain are perfectly happy because they cash in across the board with no threat to their control in the foreseeable future.

To unravel the expectations and muddy self perception takes dedication. Again and again, you will have to remember yourself as a divine spirit. This is one of the occult secrets behind jewelry and adornments. If you wear a necklace with a symbol that you associate with truth and spirit, when you become aware of it upon your neck during the course of the day it will cause you to remember yourself in this way. After doing this for some time you begin to get a wedge in through the habit wall and the first gleams of daylight will appear. From this point of observation you can achieve disconnect from foreign influence in the mind and emotional field. As each pattern arises within you and seeks to cause you to act out, your new gap of freedom allows you to remain still. Seeing the habit as being 'not you', you can trace it back to who it is from and to the moment it entered. Illuminate with understanding, and the pattern will come around but once more for its final extermination.

As the light starts to enter the body from the rejuvenating inner worlds, the soul has its first space to begin moving through. Building upon the momentum, insight gives you new impulses. Suddenly you feel like dancing instead of just walking in a straight line. You might be astonished to see the oak tree in the front yard looking back at you. You might discover a hidden ability to paint which wakes in you memories of a past life which becomes a flood of feeling. We can reincorporate every life we have ever lived with full cognizance of the abilities we had accrued through our time in any given era. We can see certain epochs of history with first hand knowledge of the aesthetic that will become a part of our character. Certain symbols will stand out and this too you can track down in the mystery of self discovery. Creativity helps you align with the flow from source and each experiment tells you a bit more about you. Reading the clues sent from your soul you can integrate all you ever were with who you are now.

Super Channeling
How to Survive Death

In order to maintain continuity of experience when dropping the physical body, attachments to the time/place events of the 3D world must be released. Anything circumstantial that is seen as part of self identity is a reduction that is not necessary from soul perspective. If you define yourself according to things such as bank account, house, car, or job, you will be lost at death, because those are solely of this world and can not be carried into the light of the astral plane.

Things you have internalized that are sourced in external machinations need to be unraveled. Trace every inner thought and inclination back from whence it derived. If you can recognize a point when input was accrued and identified with, realize that what you have found, if coming from another, can not be the essential 'you'. We will still have the brain grooves containing the knowledge at our disposal; we will just not make the mistake of believing ourselves to be this information.

We need to open the inner sensibilities that transcend the 5 body senses and our web of thoughts. With reflective awareness we can 'know'. Simultaneously experiencing all sense data and all mind potentialities, we also understand the possibilities beyond our body perception capabilities. No longer drawing immediate conclusions which shut out higher frequencies, we have a free flowing lucidity which can translate messages from a myriad of sources throughout the realms.

Practice having an easy going sense of who you are. Drop strong preferences and roll with whatever occurs. You will enjoy life more and it will happen without leaving a mark on you. Constantly move to the new in preparation for the adventure of death, the ultimate thrill ride. If you spend your incarnation building fortresses in order to attain an illusory sense of security, when death approaches, your terror will induce a deep sleep to help you deal with the process.

If you review your life now, there will be no need for it at the moment of expiration. In meditation we take the power of death into our own hands. Feeling again everything that ever happened with awareness, we put the past to rest once and for all. Then there will be no surprises to distract us when we are liberated from the body. With openness we can accept it as but another of the infinite series of events passing through our consciousness.

Super Channeling

How to Stay Centered in Hell

When the burning waves of Anger come crashing in upon you, throw open your heart; shine profoundly an inner truth which cries, "I shall not bend in my pursuit of Life's Joy and my own Eternal Salvation." Anger will split and a rainbow of light will dawn in a song which aches with the beauty of mourning loss and a healthy recovery. The newly awakened energy will be stunned at first and will then gleefully join in the celebration that has been going on in the Universe all along.

When Violence arrives with its friend Denial, thou shall not budge. Reason lends a hand to Heart backed by the resilience of Will and Clarity, relentlessly standing down haughtiness to head off the Destruction left in Violence's wake. Say, "I see you Violence and it is not okay. I know you have your reasons but they are all meant to lead me astray. I do not accept your explanation because I have one of my own. Every human being has a right to be free within their own auric field. No worldly hierarchy changes the intrinsic truth of human dignity.

When Pain puts up Walls and casts shadows upon your heart, strongly sing until the vibration of your exaltation melts the bricks like butter in the summer. Purity will bring a morning rain and transmute the Pain into Power. With Integrity you can now walk in the world bringing Grace to everything you encounter. Around your feet flowers will bloom and trees will bow to your nobility. Birds will fly around your head whistling tunes that you now know are greetings from your Mother.

Super Channeling
The Devil and the Average Person

How can a simple uninformed human stand up to the legions of darkness? They cannot. Younger souls are not yet in a position to see that they are part of the greater universal existence. They truly believe themselves to be but a small person in a local environment amongst a relatively minimal group of contacts. Trained since birth to trust the TV, their reality is carefully crafted for them by people in boardrooms who consult with mind control specialists. An average person living their family life and going to their job every day can not be expected to withstand an attack by the well researched and funded covert science of human thought manipulation.

Why are some warriors out there hammering every day on the seemingly obvious discrepancies between truth and the way society plays out their collective experience? If you are locked in the mind there is no place for the soul. And if there is no place for the soul you have lost your connection to spirit. Then a whole culture can careen wildly from one rationalization to another without the empathy and feeling that the soul provides. This is where the devil comes in to take charge of the ship for his own despotic purposes. He convinces you that a death somewhere else is not as important as the death of someone who looks like you.

Playing upon your fears and the absence of personal integrity, the devil reminds you how terrible life is…how there is danger everywhere…and how necessary it is for you to give up self-determination. Creating havoc and then saying, "Look at the havoc," the devil is full of tricks and deceptions. Waving flags and holding crosses he has no qualms about looking you right in the eye and lying. It is hard for the average person to believe that anybody would be so callous and artful in their contrivances, so they typically do not. If you look beneath the surface and realize that you have the devil in your midst, you are immediately besieged with the question, "What do we do now?"

One can't fight the devil with devilish ways or the devil will have won by making you like him. Of course anytime someone speaks truth against the devil it is turned around to seem like a condemnation of you. This is a key sign that all is not what it seems, because any being of spirit will welcome you as you are and make room for all expressions. An average person has yet to cultivate the strength to combat such a potent foe, and often succumbs because they choose to protect their tiny fiefdoms and family. Only beings that have transcended matter can live without this security as they know it is all an illusion in the first place. There is nothing to take away.

So in the end, there is the devil with his legions, and there are the human angels fighting a cosmic battle over the right for souls to enter bodies and have the freedom to develop according to nature's plan. The majority only see the surface images of what is occurring. Preferring to draw premature conclusions and somehow trying to fit everything into their own microcosmic context, they struggle on the best they can. Often angels have to battle the devil inside the average person as well as the devil himself. Stopping a contagious disease with no substance is not an easy task.

The average person isn't going to read 1000 books. They aren't going to study every culture in history and see for themselves that what is happening is just the latest flare up of the darker side of human nature. They aren't going to realize that their nation doesn't really exist and that it is all a superficial imposition. They aren't going to see the horror that everywhere they look the hand of the devil is seeking to touch your heart. So they live simple lives and look the other way. It is up to the angels to stop the madness by being sincere and bringing to the people the light of spirit. This too is contagious and eventually will disperse the shadows once and for all.

Super Channeling
Creatures of the Astral Realm

Everything that is here on Earth is in the Astral Plane. There are universities and bars, swimming holes, and super malls. There are many creatures that exist only in the 4th dimension. The closest are the ones we love to talk about in our myths. Dragons, unicorns, elves, fairies, nymphs, and all manner of entities exist just on the other side of the veil. Scoffers trapped in a limited 5 sense 1 body mentality never raise their vibration level higher than hard core 3D. Those that cultivate inner space and a meditative balance can easily raise their energy into the 4th dimension and beyond.

Coexisting with the entities of the 4th dimension you will begin to commune with them on a regular basis. The newly passed are actually very close; just out of sight. With a little practice you will be getting messages from them any time you want to let them in. Soon you will start getting flashes when you are with people. You may see a certain animal in their past lives. Many strongly take after a given animal so much so that when suggested it provokes an, "Aha!" in a room full of friends. You may also see mythological realities within some people in bodies. They will morph into something like a dwarf, a satyr, or a centaur.

There are other beings living in the 4th dimension that will be well aware of your presence in that realm. As you consciously begin to break the hold of demons over your behavior, you are actually doing psychic battle in the lower 4th dimension. Preying upon the fears and pain in people, they are actually prayed for by the people they devour. When someone is depressed or hateful, they send out the intention that draws an equivalent entity to come and exacerbate the feeling. Angels of all the colors of the rainbow plant seeds that encourage the tendency for positive actions.

Sometimes angels even battle demons to spare the weaker human. Just being an angel does not make them invincible. The demons drain them fast as well. Many angels have to learn to balance their Heart with Will so as to not be undermined in their efforts to assist humanity. The Soul of Gaia herself resonates out from the spirit of the planet to make up the dream-like world of the astral plane. Things can be manifested instantly with merely a thought, and data can be downloaded in your mind much in the way it is on Earth with computer assistance.

To attune oneself with the Sun is to be ready to lift out of the cycles of reincarnation that exist from within the context of the Earthly astral realm. Some have become aware of multiple births but then consider that to be a massive amount of time and information. In actuality the whole series of lifetimes adds experience to the soul which itself relates mainly to this solar system. You can shed even this on your way to Cosmic or Christ Consciousness. When you are aware of yourself in every atom of Existence you will see that context itself is a faulty premise. Even Love cannot contain this vastness.

Ruminations of the Universe

Super Channeling
Star Friends throughout the Universe

It is not always easy to walk the path of enlightenment. Those who tell you that it is are promoting illusions and know not of what they speak. A real master will give you a real reflection. These realities take some time to get accustomed too. As Osho and Shab say, enlightenment is instant…in fact it is already the case, but with the Minds we carry around, there will be some serious issues to deal with in bringing everything into alignment. The insights go on and on. If you are looking for a cessation of realization and a place to rest, it is best to go back to sleep and enjoy the bliss of ignorance.

Once you hear the call of truth, nothing will ever be the same. Though the Mind will again and again seek to coax you back into the shadows, stay strong in your practice. The journey is arduous, but there are many rewards along the way. The most important of which, is that whatever you find is truly yours. Those who accept ready made answers and simple systems rob themselves of everything that is most precious in life. Anyone who attempts to convince you of trite solutions to profound questions is not a friend. A friend takes responsibility for the truth and tells it to you unembellished.

As you dig deeper and deeper, you will be amazed. The mystery keeps getting more involved and the intricacies of who you are begin to be revealed. First you unravel this life…the pains and programs. You feel a freedom that previously was not even conceived of as being possible. This is only available if you get some space from the Mind and use provocations as a call to awareness instead of an excuse to take something personally and react. This is an intense discipline. You must realize that it is in your own best interest to dismantle the Ego, for it is the only way to truly make room for the Heart.

Just wait until your past lives start floating to the surface. Can you handle re-experiencing your own murder? How about being a slave, a prisoner, or feeling the loneliness of a tyrant? We have played many, many roles and to remember we have to get distance from the details, otherwise it will overwhelm us. After all, many have a hard time simply coping with this life and our current action's consequences. Seeing the grander scope of our soul's travels, we will see longer term lessons that have followed us all along. When we recover consciousness, we can finish a multitude of karmic cycles.

This is not all. We are still closer to the beginning than the end. This just brings us to who we are and what we are doing here and does not even yet get into the cosmic secrets and mysteries being whispered from one star to the next throughout the vastness of space. Some of us come from the Earth, so the plethora of lives here will be their main experience, but many of us come from other star systems. In these places, we have different bodies and exist on other planes of existence. We have many friends throughout the universe who are waiting to say hello.

Ruminations of the Universe

Super Channeling
Love for Steve Irwin

Steve Irwin was not only a likeable, sincere, and happy man who loved his life, he was also deeply spiritual in the truest sense. In tune with nature…with gratitude and enthusiasm for every day, he lived his truth. Look and see a person who is awake with an open heart. God bless him and his family. What a wonderful person and beautiful man. This world is truly better off having enjoyed the honor of his presence.

I feel he would want us to remember the messages he promoted and to give the causes real attention. See and feel the animals. Realize that they are holy and our companions through life. Don't let greedy people seeking short term gain destroy the sacredness of our planet. Make real relationships with animals and we will go a long way towards healing the Earth.

He is still with us…just on the other side. A Love like his can never disappear. I am sure he feels all of our Love and Love's us in return. Both He and We will mourn our separation. Pray that we all remember our interconnectedness and that one day we will arrive home. Always remember the good things.

Thank God.

Super Channeling

Maynard Ferguson: Still Playin'

The great jazz trumpeter Maynard Ferguson dropped in on me from the astral realms while I was folding my laundry:

"I know you thought you were done with this type of message for awhile, but since we share the horn and a love of Eastern Philosophy, it shouldn't be too surprising that I'd drop in for a visit. I can see from here that you will be able to keep space and realize who this impression is from.

I am known for playing high notes on the trumpet and that is cool. My goal was to inspire Love for music in the hearts of children and in that I was largely successful. This more so than the Hollywood glam was my soul purpose in Life.

I realized in my meditation that a devotee serves for the Joy of sharing Heart Love, and not for the temporary thrill of recognition. I had a blast on the planet and I'm still hanging around keeping an ear on things. This is a tremendously important time in human development and many of our recent arrivals are staying to watch the show.

Of note to some of you is the incomparable Steve Irwin. He is every bit the beautiful spirit here as you came to know there and believe me, he has lost nothing in the transition. If fact, here he is also very well known as a powerfully loving guardian of nature.

It is peace that you seek my friends. I'm going to get going because I have gigs here as well, but never forget that Maynard Loves you."

Super Channeling
Neanderthal, the Romantic

"Oh forgotten brothers and sisters, I hear your hearts call.

The world knows not the beauty that was in your gentle souls.

How you loved the sunset and playing together after a long day of foraging.

Never has Gaia created finer beings than you.

You respected nature and were thankful for her gifts.

You expressed this gratitude in art and song.

How you loved to discover new wonders around each and every turn.

You are remembered by your Mother."

Ruminations of the Universe

Super Channeling
A Galaxy of Gossip

What is it that people find interesting? I could speak of doom and demons and many would delight. Both are real factors that we face as we move forward in the evolution of humanity. Doom is the point of view cultivated by demons. Absence of soul light within leaves empty space for influence by a demon. They are drawn by the hurts and misconceptions which keep the soul out of most bodies. There is an aspect that is the embodiment of our denial and there is an aspect that is an outside manifestation. We break the connection when we heal our pain.

Some people respond well to the idea of Angels and God. How many have actually communicated mind to mind with an Angel or felt the Love of God in their own hearts? There are Angels that make up one general color area of the spectrum and Arch Angels which harmonize the whole rainbow of light. There are many gods and one creative force which sustains all things. Aum the vibration can be tuned into and all mysteries of the Universe can be revealed. Sure we can go to this Spirit Guide or that Ascended Master, but if we go right to the Source, we know everything from the inside out.

When you see the plan of Creation, do you need to micromanage the construction of a single building? There is a force which drives latent potential to become actualized. If you allow for it, it may turn and greet you with a smile. If you look deeply enough into any living thing you will see the holy spirit reflected back to you. When your spirit meets another's you will see that they are one and the same. That twinkle in the eye is the juice of life. The joke is the magic behind the solidity we mistakenly crystallize in our own mind. It is just the mind's tendency to perceive a flow in chunks.

There is the physical world and there is the astral world which is a more fluid fantastic version of the physical in the land of light and ideas. Most people that pass from this world go to this astral realm and rest in the relaxation that comes with being free of the density of the physical body. Pattern integrity remains intact and when you cross over you can visit a loved one as easily as walking down the street and knocking on a door. With just a thought you can draw a loved one near. If you are aware of the astral realm while in the physical you can operate there as well as here.

Beyond the astral realm, which is sustained by the love and gravitational force of Gaia the Mother, is the land of Wholeness. Eventually all Souls who seek liberation unite with the Father, the Sun (Ra, Helios, Apollo). Our Father who Art in the

Heavens, will share with us as much information as we can allow in. You will see the whole story of human civilization, and intuitively receive the complete history of the solar system. When you transcend even this, you will be able to use the Sun as a portal to connect to other stars. Then, the whole Galaxy of Gossip is suddenly available for your edification.

Ruminations of the Universe

Super Channeling
Zeta Power

The Zetas operate on frequencies that overlap our own. The edges of their world do not exist in ours. They are in the lower reaches of the 4th dimension. You must understand that there are beings of all kinds throughout the realms. The ones we see and document are those that are closest. Some speak to our intuition and some try to control our mind. It is truly a crowded arena. Individual integrity is of utmost importance. Declare autonomy and empower your aura's light. Humanity is transcendent because of its ability to bring in the soul.

The Zetas do not have the soul possibilities that the humans do. This is why they are crossbreeding with us and tinkering so much with DNA. They are trying to crack the code of life. What they don't understand in the least is the realm of heart. It is love that they are missing. They have witnessed it as a phenomenon and documented it extensively but they have no experience of it. There has been some success with the experiments that have been done and not all humans have been unwilling. Some are happy to let it fly and see what happens.

The Zetas are playing a role in politics as a go

between for the reptilians. It is not always easy for reptilians to keep their shape in this world. Zetas have an easier time of it. Their most commonly used technology erases the recent memory of the person they are working with. A few they let remember and a few they can not control. It is in the reproductive organs that the Zetas are lacking. Think of the concept of shame for the Japanese and apply it to the Zetas 10-fold. They can enjoy intimacy and feel fulfillment through friendship.

The Zetas are able to communicate telepathically and so have hive-like tendencies. They can block the thoughts of others but this immediately gives rise to suspicion in the others. The analogy of doctors or scientists is somewhat apt for most of their activities. Occasionally they will break to watch the stars or converse briefly about some event that occurred. There is a hierarchy that seems to form spontaneously. Mostly it is based on experience and the practicality of performing a given function.

Super Channeling
Overflowing Joy of the Soul

You are here on the Earth. There is just a little time left to realize the greater continuity of your soul being. Many lives come and go tied just to location and environment. A few bright lights come along with the ability to rise above this self concept. Realizing the life pulse within, they become a part of the universe. They always were, but now they know it. Their breath and their heart beat are one with the eternal celebration. All music comes from this source and all experience is meant to lead you here.

Wake up sleepy dreamer. At first it is painful to proceed, but the glimpses of sunlight sustain you on your journey. Soon you begin to live what you had seen in your peak moments of insight. You are pleasantly surprised to find that expansion and growth goes on and on. Each time you settle in there is more on the way. Delighting in truth, the seeker breaks down all barriers and restores their soul to its greater glory. Freedom of consciousness while in the body is the most magnificent of miracles.

It is tricky to realize how belief actually limits you, but it does. When you are fixated on one thing, you rule out others. This is not necessary when all things are possible. Each interpretation takes you away from the actual. Every association puts something extra between you and the truth. Get back to the mind you had when you were born. Float there and observe. Let the 'Eye' reflect reality. Imagination will fill in the details later. Whatever you do, don't let doubt rob you of the gifts that are rightfully yours.

We must slip into a slightly altered mode of communication to get past preconceptions and speak to the soul in a language it understands. Before becoming incarnate you had a plan for the lessons you thought would be beneficial in this life. Nothing can be certain, so you chose the conditions which you thought would provoke what you needed to learn. Situations are presented and when you finally make good courageous choices, you can move on. This also happens in your dreams. Much is the help you are provided.

Several thousand people on Earth and several hundred thousand angels, gods, guides, and ascended masters on the astral plane are attending to the project of ascension. Those of you who are a part of this will feel the inner call to be active in promoting this revelation both in words and deeds. Each moment becomes an opportunity to show grace and wisdom. The ultimate service is to your own inner nature. Cultivating 'God's plan in you,' sets free the heart song and the overflowing joy which serves others.

Ruminations of the Universe

Super Channeling
Qualities of an Awakened Soul

Being near them puts you at ease. You will feel more like yourself and relax in a way that is profound. It will be invigorating, and there might well be frequent bursts of laughter. There will most certainly be empathy. You will be treated with honor because an awakened soul honors the life within every creature every moment. Aware of their place on planet Earth, they never forget that their home is in the stars. Getting past the first stage of perception revolving around the 5 senses and the body, they have reconnected with their more subtle inner energies. In time, most can do this if they are open and sincere in their search.

They have a quality of timelessness. You will not be sure if they are 30, 300, or 3000 years old, because they speak in terms of the ultimate. While others sleep or go through their daily routines, the awakened soul is considering how to contribute to the growth of humanity and how to make it easier for other souls who are approaching the threshold of realization. There are a percentage of the people which resonate with the message of transcendence. It is the truth that life goes on beyond the body and mind. It is a realization that the seeker must be ready for and accept willingly. It is an initiation into a whole new paradigm.

An awakened soul rarely plays roles. They do not change who they are to accommodate circumstance. Uniqueness and originality is their very being and they have learned to stand behind it. Their actions exhibit grace and there will be poetry in their motion. They will tend to be good listeners and when they in turn express to another, it may leave them feeling spaced out. These souls bring intelligence and artistry to everything they do. They might compose music, paint pictures, tell stories, or do anything creative to express Love in the world of forms. Planting seeds all over, they make the subconscious a greener place.

They know they are made of energy and light. While living in the 3D world, they also live in the 4th and many make it to the 5th Dimension. Here you can freely communicate telepathically with the Sun and Angels. Reclaiming past lives and frozen soul trauma, the aspirant gives birth to themselves anew. This is a major spiritual milestone. After experiencing all of this information and then letting it go, the imprint of the truth it has for you now will be left and you will have rejoined the deeper meaning of your life path. You can now consciously live in truth and it is up to you what happens as you proceed. After all, you are the creator.

Ruminations of the Universe

Transcendence

Transcendence
A Warrior Monk's Way

Judicious with the sword, a warrior monk may also choose to swing away if the circumstance in the moment calls for it. Action in tune with Source begets no Karma. God on the Ground, each step is an opportunity for meditation and to demonstrate Tao in the flesh. There is no moral code…more an intuitive sense of Virtue and standing for Truth. The Earth itself may tremble, but the monk's way is steady…not of this world. Something from the beyond compels the warrior forward through good times and hardship. Rather than mind, it is with Heart that he leads.

Ripping asunder all that would bind, the Lion-Hearted hero walks on. Giving everything due consideration, he makes decisions based on what is best for all, and moves on. Constantly monitoring for Ego influence, the Warrior keeps the channel clean at all times. Moving with inspiration, the Creator's Will works through him. We all are One, not just in a philosophic sense, but in a constant vibrant vibratory interconnectedness that is easy to perceive if you are able to come to rest and open your inner sensibilities. Aum is a wave of friendship and a beacon to the Way.

Conclusions are not a luxury a Warrior Monk can afford. Things swirl and take new fleeting forms. Preconceptions are no longer there and interpretations do not follow. Holding the energies with Awareness and Presence, the sannyasin allows the Holy Spirit and gives this Creative force a chance to express itself fully. This is when everything really starts to hum and the monk is no longer a monk, but a conduit for the Word. It is like talking to Existence itself. The only question that remains is how open you can be to this Voice.

Certainty is not a thing to be desired. Rigidity of Mind holds even the most intelligent back. It is a missing link from the Western approach. This of course is why the mission given to me upon my Heart by the Creator is to find every means possible to insert aspects of Eastern Wisdom into our Cultural paradigm. It isn't hard to do as analogous examples are everywhere. What makes better sense than an Angel Buddha? We shouldn't be against anything other than limitation. Accepting all, we have so many colors to play with as we paint anew upon the canvas of life.

With one hand on the wheel and the other gripping my pen, I ride through the storms and stresses of my own journey. It is in Love that I share with humanity. Naturally I am compelled to sing my song to the wind. It is such a beauty to do. The river sometimes sends you down unexpected tributaries. Most likely it is to meet a friend. Women and men, animals, and all of Creation in harmony; this is the hope of Peace. To some it may seem unrealistic and this is fine! They are doing their skeptical thing. Leave the future to us dreamers and we shall welcome you home.

Ruminations of the Universe

Transcendence
Hitler's Curse

What's happening out there folks? I would love to avoid politics and move on to writing mostly about meditation and the wonderful spiritual traditions of the world, but when they keep shoving lies up my ass, what is a guy to do? I should say, what is a guy who is awake with responsibility towards life, humanity, and where we are all going to do? After all millions of people don't do a damn thing, absolutely convinced that as long as they do their little jobs and shop, shop, shop, the problems of the world do not have anything to do with them. Maybe it is Hitler's curse and we are all experiencing what it is like to be in a bunker with the world crashing down around us.

To peruse the news (hey that would make a good web site – 'peruse the news') makes the head spin. Voters clearly denounced the wars of aggression in the only real action most believe they have to take. Even the bi-partisan Iraq geezer group's essential message was that America has to get out of Iraq soon. World leaders, the UN, historical Allies, and a vast majority of the people of the US all say the same thing. The future of America is being traded so that a small group of people can build permanent bases in the Middle East so they can control the oil. What the events transpiring at this time make all too clear is that the current leaders do not give care one to the needs of the people.

It is a brazen approach to twist the vote from a mandate to pull back troops, to a massive troop increase in Iraq! Even now they are forcing soldiers to stay for multiple tours of duty and draining our reserves to the point of complete exhaustion. If anything like Katrina were to happen again, who will be left to assist the people who are supposedly being protected by attacking a country on the other side of the world!? It is twisted logic, but since most Americans have no philosophical center, they can go farther and farther out on a limb with their justifications. Those who say that America has left God out of the equation are correct, but absolutely not the Christian/Jewish grandpa in the sky!

The authoritarian boss archetype has been the Western world's worst nemesis. Whether it is a judgmental God, or a judgmental dictator, either way this is the opposite of life and could truly be called anti-Christ. Make no doubt that this is an Old Testament related poison that has permeated into the dark corners of the collective subconscious. There is no longer any time to mince words, or be kind about it. It is simply not true. Maybe when humans were closer to barbarians they needed basic order so a ruse was concocted by Moses in the desert to keep the stragglers in line, but through this approach, the best of humanity, it's divinity, will never have the Love it needs to flower.

Almost everything has been politicized, so even taking pen to paper (or in this case keyboard to word processor) begins your participation in the debate for the destiny of the human species. Do not attempt this if you are not ready to take the heavy assaults that come with questioning the powers that be. Luckily some Americans are discovering the truth through the internet and other sources of media. It just hasn't translated into reality on the ground. One reason is that the Americans who have a clue are still a vast minority. Even the decent, semi-neutral, educated middle class basically knows nothing but the tales they were told in their text books. They still crap their pants when questioned.

What is it that is the major hurdle to actually making a change of some sort? Fear! I'll never forget the atmosphere in the air just as W. was about to make his disastrous charge into Iraq. I never believed any of the BS. It felt wrong from the second W. bumbled into the Oval office. My intuition always told me his words were lies. He was really revealing his own darkness and blaming others for it, a classic psychological illness of people in rabid denial. The few people speaking up were skewered. Has America apologized to Scott Ritter for calling him a traitor? Who is the traitor now? Is speaking the truth the work of a traitor, or is sinking the whole American experiment in a sickening display of self-aggrandizement?

America should line her shores with wind machines, and sink the money that is being spent killing tens of thousands of innocent people into solar panels. Then there would be no need to take from the weak. How much more anti-Christ can you get then that? Unfortunately the US is operating from a might makes right approach, not an educated and thoughtful one. Until someone with a heart is elected, there will never be a solution that works. Right now peace means war, and victory could mean total defeat. As the dollar sinks with the world's reaction to the horrors they see, what will this bring for the simple folks on the ground?

Don't be surprised when you realize that you have slowly been put in a cage. It may not have physical bars (yet), but if you can't speak out loud what you feel, what kind of a life are you living?

Transcendence

Have you bowed your head to forces that you fear? Do you go along to get along and try not to 'rock the ship of state'? Give me a break. This country was meant to have vigorous honest debates with nothing off limits. Newt wants to take your free speech away, because there is no other way to completely dominate your mind. Anyone who thinks McCain, Guiliani, or any of the other cronies won't continue the awful course we are on is simply kidding themselves.

Generation X, it is up to you. Chart a new course and assert what you believe. There is still time, but we have to stop the Baby Boomers from destroying the world right now. They are not leaders, thinkers, or healthy humans. They are still reacting to the trauma that the 'greatest generation' inflicted on them by killing all of their real leaders. Do you think any of those assassinated by the shadows would support this crap? JFK, RFK, MLKJ, and Lennon would be leading the charge. Actually if they would have lived, none of this probably would have ever happened. The greats of Generation X are out there. It is time to speak now or forever hold your peace 6 feet under ground.

Ruminations of the Universe

Transcendence
Occult Forces of WW3

There is much below the surface game that plays itself out on television sets across the world. Skewed reports from hither and thither barely tell us a slice of what is actually going on. Front men dress up in costumes and dance around to distract us while the brutality continues unabated. Instinct once again outweighs civility and the pandora's box of chaos has been unleashed. The equilibrium of world affairs has been thrown off and it is inevitable that one day balance must be restored.

A lot has been made of the comparison between Bush and Hitler. Having lived both in Hitler's Germany (past life), and Bush's America, I can tell you that they are quite different. What Bush is doing is using the control techniques of Hitler as studied and translated by Rove, Cheney, and Rummy. It is blatantly obvious, from the language expressing the "will of providence" to the overt use of symbols/catch phrases to influence the subconscious. Bush himself said he has to repeat the same trite phrases over and over to "catapult the propaganda".

You could almost go page by page through Mein Kampf and point to the talking points. The difference however is that there is nothing but control from Bush. Hitler's controlling ways were put in service of his whacky but intricate philosophy. He was basically "for" the German people, and before things took a turn for the worse in 1942, things had never looked better from their perspective. The same can not be said for Bush's America. Infrastructure is crumbling, health care is out of reach for many, the middle class is disappearing, unchecked immigration is tearing the country apart from the inside…. The list seems never ending.

We can believe that Bush is losing power now, but he has already set some very dangerous events into motion. Even being the intellectual midget that he is, he sometimes gives off a terrifying vibration, and then you can be sure that he is channeling dark forces that have their own agenda on the planet. Those of you who Love Christ should be appalled at what Bush is doing in His name. There is no rationalization that can hide the piles and piles of civilian corpses he is leaving laying in the dust across the world. Just because phony Tony stands next to him and hawks such as Hannity, Newt and Netanyahu say again and again it is ok, does not make it so.

We each are personally responsible for the role we play in the Earth's transition to a new phase of existence. There is no way back and the destruction will be in direct proportion to our ability to stand up and learn the lessons we are meant to learn in this time. Are we going to be like babies and say, "Out of sight, out of mind," or are we going to have the ability to see the gestalt and realize that all things are interconnected? Are we going to pretend in our little minds that those painted as "evil doers" are not human beings and therefore can be killed indiscriminately? This mentality is exactly what has led to every holocaust throughout history, including the one that took place in the Americas not so long ago. If settlers would have befriended and incorporated some of the wisdom of the native peoples, history could have taken a much more benign course.

The bellicosity of the Islamic leaders shows a combination of the voice of the oppressed and the imitation thereof by prop boogey men to justify even further aggression. This distinction should be made clear. How is it that the American populace can see movie after movie where fantastic special effects portray anything the imagination can dream up, and yet they do not connect this ability to the shabby little videos they see on the official state sponsored news programs? A regime could make up anything and seemingly prove it so! This is almost as dangerous as the weapons of war themselves, if not more so because it corrupts the soul of the people.

Unstoppable will is only necessary when you are charting a course opposed to nature, otherwise no effort to sustain would be necessary. No matter how locked in a person is to their course of action, they will eventually wear themselves out and start to become extremely unbalanced. While Bush is destroying the future of the nation, exhausting our treasure, and letting the homeland crumble, he drones on and on the same phrases. Is anybody still paying attention? Unfortunately some people, including supposedly intelligent news people act as if hearing the same thing for the 100th time is an original answer. It is not and should be addressed directly.

Whether it be Judaism (5000+ years old), Christianity (2000+ years old), or Islam (1500+ years old), the face of fanaticism is distorted and ugly. The philosophical/cultural world paradigm can shift far away from these echoes of the past. Science and mysticism have come together and revealed what actually IS. Anybody can deprogram themselves and see this with their own eyes. As eclectic forces battle to steal your heart and mind, declare personal independence.

Transcendence

Find for yourself the truth of Life on Earth. Speak to God through your own personal connection called Intuition. Have Faith that if you believe in yourself, you will find your own way.

Ruminations of the Universe

Transcendence
Cult of Cash and the Dogma of Dollars

There is nothing more warping to a soul than to place the value of material possessions above matters of the spirit. When attempting to figure out why the world is so lost, and why America is careening out of control, one has to look no further than the almighty dollar. More than anything, Americans are taught to value things. The God that is worshipped by many is money. Do you think there is not a subconscious impact to the words IN GOD WE TRUST being printed right on the circulating paper itself? The implication is that the money is God and if you spend your life scrounging for it, you will be 'secure'. Faith need not apply, because the Capitalist system is there for you. From Health care to 401K, you do not even need to bother with the risk of living! Just do as you are told and everything will be fine.

Some may even agree with this assessment in theory, but in day to day life they cannot escape money's influence on their thinking and choices. The collective reinforcement is everywhere. This is one reason why the people working to cut down on public billboards and advertisements philosophically have a correct idea. Being immersed in manipulations, our gestalt mindset is dramatically altered. After awhile we become so accustomed to it, that we can be SOLD just about anything. For example: a War on Terror, or a War on Iraq. The White House did nothing different than any PR firm trying to launch an ad campaign. Propaganda is the name of the game. Truth is not the measure of success, influence for financial gain is. We may consider that as a country we lost billions on war, but not everybody did.

In fact much of what occurred is a shifting of the nation's money into the accounts of corporations and the dramatically dreary families of privilege. The situation was not instigated by the individuals currently dwelling in bodies participating in the scenario. They were born into an elitism established by their forefathers at the expense of natives, slaves, women, and poor whites. America pretends there is no class system but in fact it is one of the most diabolical in all of history. It is a 300 million tiered class structure based on what is in your bank account. How the money gets there is irrelevant as long as you are not caught. If you have it there are different rules for you. Much praise will follow you and there is danger that you will begin to see interpersonal relationships as just another business transaction.

So obsessed do people become with greed and the desire to accumulate wealth, they lose track of all that is truly meaningful in life. A person can share a few supportive words, or a hug of love and it can melt away years of pain. Giving a gift from the heart for no reason other than that you feel called to share is the real indulgence on Earth. Taking at the expense of others, you may become richer in the world, but you will become poor in spirit. Minds under the influence of this deception can not see beauty, refinement, or grace. This is why in America art, music, poetry, and philosophy are not integrally valued. They are intangibles of the soul. Their worth is transcendent, incomparable, and limitless! You can not use them to go to Wal-Mart and buy a flat screen TV. You can however save your soul and heal your heart.

A great reorientation has to occur if America is ever to be truly tremendous. Christianity has become intermingled with Capitalism to create a mish mash of illusions and consciousness traps. Stop crucifying Jesus, and free the Father as thou shall have no other Gods before Him (especially not money). This is not an obligation, but in our own best interest. If we worship other than the creative force which sustains the universe and gives us our inherent goodness, we will be swayed to walk off the path of righteousness into the thorns of sin as defined by the cause and effect penalties inherent in straying from the Tao. To be in harmony with nature is easy and right. To be isolated and fight to gain selfish power is to eventually become exhausted and render this and many lifetimes detrimental to the growth of humanity.

Always keep space from the ways/wars of the world. You can move amongst the masses and buy trinkets in the marketplace. Enjoy and if you have money, spend it guilt free. Just keep it in its proper perspective. Do not let it influence your personal value system. Love and Life are worth far more than the Dogma of Dollars. There are universal laws with rewards from a much sweeter source. If there is anything that America needs to wake up to it is that consumerism is not a healthy way of life. It is not to be praised, cultivated, or desired. If you are involved in perpetuating this disease, you have personal responsibility. The line is crossed when the truth is obscured and a gift becomes an obligation. Remember that you are always intimately tied to the whole. To be for all is to be for your highest self and for God.

Transcendence
Expressing Will

Many of the people who consider themselves spiritual are actually cutting off their source with a hyper-morality that makes even Christianity seem innocuous in comparison. Referring to each other in only the most glowing of terms, they are polarized to such an extent that reality is left far behind. Boxing themselves and each other into a tiny corner of rose colored words, anything that doesn't fit in to their preconceptions is judged with a ferocity that would make the promoters of the twin tablets of stone envious. The most dangerous aspect is that they take the language of love and use it to manipulate others. Collectively shunning dissenters they consider their own perspective above and beyond all else. They consider it only a matter of time until everybody else sees the light and agrees with their version of events.

The most dangerous thing to souls entering the body is the denial imposed by the world. The sprouting bud of spirit is tender and sensitive. The ways of the world are harsh and numbing. Again and again the truth will seem an affront to those bound by habit so they will attempt to push the soul back out and control the other's behavior in response. The soul longs for justice and is repeatedly betrayed by others who are self centered and oblivious to the greater universe. The pain builds over time and that part of you which never had a voice needs to find itself and express in totality what it is feeling. This is the Kundalini and a gift of our Mother the Earth. Do you think this crushed aspect of the soul is not going to be upset or angry for having been denied the right of existence?

Deprogramming is one thing and finding your power is another. The first thing that controllers claim is that expressing feminine energy is being negative. Take note! Extensive observation proves repeatedly that this is an early resistance that the birthing soul has to overcome. Care not what is said and how you are seen. Do what you have to do to make room for your soul to enter the world. Be willing to sacrifice all social interests, because a great reorganization has to occur. Soon you will see who your real friends are, and who has simply been using you as a means to their own end. Be ready for the guilt trips and the expectations. Even watch for them to continue playing the game, including you even though you aren't there! One favorite trick to draw you back in to drama is to act like your stepping out of madness is a conflict that needs to be resolved. Sometimes a person needs to walk away and stay away.

If you want to be here alive as a soul, you need to roar with an expression that shakes the foundations of all rigid concepts. We are a fluid process that gets stopped up by the demands of humans upon one another. Life on Earth is natural and easy. All that we feel resistance towards is perpetuated upon the surface by the Zombies who know not what they do. We can be like Christ and forgive them but that does not mean we have to spend our precious time with them. They will fry the circuits and keep the flower from blooming. Find an environment that cultivates the truth of who you are. If you can't find one, take the heroic step of creating one and offering your oasis to others. Everybody doesn't have to like you or agree with what you are doing. The relief of recovering your lost fragments through powerful expression makes possible the fruits to come.

Ruminations of the Universe

Transcendence
Build an Alternative Approach to Life

Have we passed the point of complacency to where we openly acknowledge the brutality being committed in the name of God and country while choosing to simply go about our own business? Making each minor adjustment necessary for our own life to accommodate increasing restriction, we dig a deeper and deeper hole where the cries of our fellow human beings on the other side of the globe are nothing more than an echo of something in the dark reaches of our subconscious. The heart gets closed out because it is the only way to carry on such an existence. The view gets narrower and narrower to just the tiniest of slivers. Intolerance of dissent grows, and the fanatical radicals draw a big circle around their kind and look at everybody else as the enemy.

Take no notice of the camera on the corner. Don't worry about the blackmail potential of a government or corporation that has tracked every click you have ever made on the internet (past included). Keep saying that the other guy is bad when he gets spirited away for a no-trial crucifixion; it is the best way to keep them from coming for you. It is not so surprising that scape-goating can happen on a grander scale then simply that of a domestic domicile. Just like an abusive household where a know-it-all dad harms his family and then blames anyone who speaks up, this country is in a vicious psychological trap with a plentitude of enablers. Standing up for truth and resisting the entropy of denial is the way to remain an autonomous sovereign individual.

Why this type of person is becoming more and more of a scarcity is a quirk of history. You would think that together as a civilization we would continue to make progress, but consider that in every war that has occurred, the loser's philosophy gets just about totally banned. War after war, there are now dozens of groups whose philosophies are completely thrown out. Is it really true that the loser of every war's platform was 100% wrong? Sometimes millions believed in an idea to the point of sacrificing everything, but history will erase the sincerity of their convictions because due to circumstance, they ended up on the losing side of a struggle. With fewer and fewer thought options, the potential for the full expression of human evolution gets squeezed out.

Going about their pre-programmed habits, many repeat the same cycles until dropping the body. Emotions and love do not necessarily arise as a part of everybody's incarnation experience. Substitutions with similar nomenclatures replace the actual experience for one who has been cut off from their essential divine nature. What is the best way to instigate this desperate state of affairs? Teach the ancient belief systems and lock the young into support of your personal positions. Then they are finished before they ever begin. Later a world of 50 year old juveniles will insist that their way is the only way and that they are never incorrect. Any who would seek to show them the obvious error of their ways will be attacked as the one creating problems.

This is possible because the former basics of humanity have been almost erased from our cultural paradigm. Art, music, and philosophy are buried and made to be untenable careers. Selling poison pills is a much more honorable profession in this society. There is never a lack of positions in the field of advertising…always remember sex sells. One who questions the status quo will be shamed, while one who gets "involved" in supporting their local political worshipper of death will be praised. "Get those enemies" is proclaimed without the understanding that what they are fighting is their own inner demons. Projecting their unacknowledged wounds, they prove themselves correct by creating that which they fear. It is best to steer clear of the carnage.

Find your friends, and get to work on building an alternative approach to life.

Transcendence
The Cost of Truth

In a society as full of propaganda and illusion as the one we currently live in, the world is turned upside down and inside out. 1000's are killed in the name of 'freedom' and human rights are disappearing one by one. It seems ludicrous to one who is informed, but it is truly scary how many actually believe in it. Of course we as humanity have not yet figured out that the quickest way to take freedom is in the name of freedom. Those trapped in the mind can be controlled so easily.

Try telling a few of them that they are Christians due to various historical quirks, not the least of which is the guilt of the murderous Roman Emperor Constantine. Throw them a few facts about their hero Lincoln's killing of the Indians and burning down of towns. Suggest that perhaps the stories they were told in elementary school are not the whole of history. Being the bearer of truth may well put you directly in the line of fire.

Members of your family and co-opted friends could turn their back on you and blame you as if you are always being 'negative'. They can justify it in their own minds because bringing up realities such as the hundreds of thousands of innocent Iraqi lives being taken and of course, you hate America. How dare you disturb their cherished illusions? It is atrocious that you would appeal to the conscience and empathy that they don't have!

When you do not go with the status quo, even your very existence seems an offence to them. There is nothing more threatening than an individual who will not play along. Why has the society always taken revenge on the brightest among us? It is quite likely that those who wrap their deeds in Christianity would not stand for the presence of Christ. He would disturb their deception and he might even speak up for the under represented. Off to crucifixion again.

This is precisely why so many do not give voice to their perceptions. They do not want to be viciously attacked, so they just eek along in silence trying to stay out of the way. This is a form of psychic imprisonment. As Bob Marley said, "No chains around my feet, but I'm not free." Truth is literally discriminated against. It could hurt your chances of getting or keeping a job and leave you isolated in your circumstance. Often what you get in return for reminding the world of their denial is scorn.

What is good in it? Why live truthfully and dig out the hidden reality that is locked behind a collective mental prison? To free your soul! As long as you believe in mind stuff you will never have any space in your body for the soul to enter in. Rigidly holding to fixed ideas is the quickest way to kill your own heart and reinforce this condition in others. It is a spiritual emergency as this disease is spreading like wildfire with the flames being fanned by those who seek to control the whole world.

There is no other way to get back to the reality of life on Earth than to unravel that which has infiltrated our minds from the outside. Some of it may have even been delivered by others who thought they were doing us a favor. This is part of the program. Can you see the cold hard truths? Can you set free the deeper meaning of incarnation? Can you find your own divinity before it is too late? It is time to look these questions in the eye and reevaluate the situation we find ourselves in.

There is no ideology more sacred than any another because they all exist only in the mind of man and are intrinsically false. What would you discover if you were the first being who arrived on the planet and there was nobody else to tell you what to believe? Most likely you would observe nature, take delight in the sunlight, and begin to express your own creative role in the Universe. Until we get back to this basic harmony with Life, the suffering will go on and on.

Transcendence
Perils of the 'American' Mind

For one who seeks truth beyond all things and longs for their own connection to the Source, they will find America a chaotic wilderness of barren philosophy. Most make every decision from their Ego; in other words they are concerned with merely their own desires. Their reckoning doesn't include any but the most immediate of relatives. This is what is perpetuated as 'family values'. As long as they have what they need, they care not for anyone outside of their sphere. Rushing to get their presents from Wal-Mart (made in China which is about to sink the US economy), wars in a foreign land are barely on their radar.

If you are minding your own life in peace, it will be just a matter of time before one of the 'Americans' crashes into you and one way or another starts to put pressure on you either subtly or overtly to become more like them. Understanding not the ways of faith, they assure you that your life would be much better if filled with a million stresses like theirs. *'How could you be right when you put Faith above the dollar? Don't you realize that money makes the world go 'round? How can you have the luxury of looking at the stars while we are all out rushing to get nowhere? You need saving and for your own good we will do it by force if we must!'*

Another of the amazing things is that with absolutely no study of the human condition they put their opinion not only equal to, but above someone who has actually spent their life in meditation and the pursuit of knowing as opposed to belief. (If you are in another country, I can tell you for certain that most any American feels vastly superior to you. At best they feel that you will 'get it' about the great American way eventually.) A person of real understanding goes so far past the masses, that they have no connecting point. Tao is not a belief system it is a way of life. It does not accommodate Americanism, or any other 'ism' for that matter. It is the truth that is right in front of your eyes. It needs no convincing or spin to be sustained.

I have no doubt that the truth seekers among you have difficulties with the 'Americans'. They will push you and then if you tell them to back off and respect your divine right as a human, they will attack you as if you committed the act of aggression. *'How dare you suggest that they don't have the right to invade your space and push you in the direction of their own mind control! And to express your feelings instead of repressing them like the rest… Sheer blasphemy!!!'* You will be scorned, shunned, and avoided like the plague if you have the tenacity and wherewithal to remain with the truth and keep professing it come what may. This leads us to another point about the 'Americans'.

Even if they don't externally claim this as the case, all but the fewest of the few are completely Christianized. This has been a process cranking away for so long that it is practically coded in their DNA. This is why spirits from the East have traveled or incarnated in the West, to get a foothold for the ideas that could cure this madness. You must understand that if 9 out of 10 people in the room are Christian, even the one who is not will begin to shape their values around those of the other people. Thus, Christianity once removed. All the TV shows and the default national conversation mistakenly takes this as a given.

One thing both Republicans and Democrats can agree on is the glory of their savior Jesus Christ! Maybe they put that aside for a moment when they are taking money from the Jewish lobby, but then the Good Book can be the blanket they all wrap themselves up in and parade around to the masses. Try being a Zen monk in America sometime. It takes great Will and determination not to let them corrupt you. Unfortunately all the time you spend holding them back is time not spent being creative. If you relate to these words, bless you for all you are trying to do for Life. When we are all back on the astral plane we can have a big party to say, "I told you so."

Transcendence
Sensation Nation

Americans just can not get enough cerebral titillation. If there isn't anything going on, you can be sure it will be mere moments before something rushes in to fill the vacuum. The 24 hour news cycle's most important job is to make sure we never get a rest from human tragedy and despair. We are trained to need stimulation, occupation, and sedation. Filling every second of our lives with 'stuff' there is no time for us to be at rest and reflect upon who we are inside. The effort to avoid fear on the outside exacerbates the fear we feel on the inside and fans the infernos of humanity's long time nemesis, hatred of each other.

Our lexicon is augmented by the War Machine and terms like 'Shock and Awe' and 'Surge' are now threaded through every day conversations. Somehow we become disconnected from the original death and carnage sewed by these extreme uses of force and are amazed when we reap the results of these poor choices. America acts like a 'cool' kid from high school who refuses to relent on pressing this false self image. It would rather die than change course, it is so identified with the path that it is on. To grow or evolve is mistaken as defeat because wisdom is not used as the measure of success, but rather unfortunately the perpetuation of limited ideology is the standard.

One of the main reasons Americans can not see beyond the end of their noses is their obsession with the religion of Christianity. So many of them absolutely believe that Jesus is the only way to heaven and that if you don't follow him, they are doing you a favor by trying to cram it down your throat. The veneer of sophistication leads them to think they are somehow different from the 'enemy' who is doing exactly the same thing under another disguise. Far be it for most Christians to crack a history book, they whistle 'Dixie' when you bring up such inconvenient points as the gospels being written well after the fact, Jesus being voted as God in a board meeting, and that nobody would even be a Christian if it wasn't for the murderous emperor Constantine imposing Christianity upon a crumbling Roman Empire.

Constantly reinforcing each other's illusions, they create an alternate reality. Boxing themselves into smaller and smaller often contradiction laden spaces, they can not rectify the discrepancy so they start eating pills by the handful. Money to the church, money to the government, money to the pharmacy, and the list goes on… It is a bureaucracy of confusion that each person has to try to sort out just to get through the day. Work, work, work for things that are not necessary and only end up harming mental and eventually physical health. I guess this helps when they shake you down once again at the hospitals (if they don't just turn you away and leave you to die because you could not afford insurance).

Come back to peace my friends. As they say in Zen, sitting silently doing nothing, the grass grows by itself. The whole disaster is superfluous and unnecessary to the blessing of life. When we see wars rage, it is not something to be for or against. It is something to understand and heal. All sides are in a bad way and hurting. One must not gain at the cost of another. It does not need to work that way. Together we can create systems that benefit everybody and the synergy of Love will be the joy of the Earth.

Transcendence
Mind Madness and Soul Suicide

Trapped in the mind there is madness. The imprint is so deep that unless you have gained some ground in past lives, you will probably not escape the threshold. Luckily there are many old souls around cultivating peace in a land of war. Sometimes the word, "peace" conjures wimpy notions, but nothing could require more strength and determination. Resisting the impulse to fall into the habits of the unconscious, one has to suffer their attacks when you no longer play their game. You will be surprised to find that people you once thought were close to you are shadows undermining your Will at every turn. One seeking salvation must galvanize a wholeness of being that can remain un-swayed when offered a change to sink into the morass of commonality and lack of integrity.

It is interesting how some resonate with a certain type of language and others run from it like it is a death blow. It is indeed very murderous, but only to misconception. Simple words of truth can be feared more than the physical reality of dropping bombs on humans. Tell a Neo-Con supporter about the innocents and naturally they will attack you. Remind them that their vote endorses carnage and they will act like you are a pariah uncomfortable to be around. Excuse me but, "It is reality and just because you hide your head in the sand of your own sense pleasures, does not mean that your actions or inactions are inconsequential." When war is declared on you personally, to simply give in to avoid stirring the waters is a type of soul suicide.

War seems to be a favorite TV show for some and nothing more. Maybe they will want to change the channel when a bomb is shoved up their own ass. We will never find a resonant harmony on the world stage until every last denied expression is given a chance to be aired out. True freedom of speech gives society room to breathe so that no suppression builds up. False leaders gain strength from enforced suppression by playing on its fears. It is impossible to chop the world up into pieces. All and everything must be accepted as being there and having a right to exist. When this reaches a saturation point, an amazing thing will occur. The old pains will begin to be transformed. The lost energy crying in pain and frozen in space, can now flow towards creativity.

Things can never be settled by force or by specific ideology. Even the rosiest of scenarios becomes a prison because of its innate conceptual limitation. Think of all the slivers of perception being offered out there: Christianity, Islam, Republican, Neo-

Transcendence

Con, Democrat, Socialism... Politics or religion, there is really not much of a difference. Each seeks to stake out the territory of the mind and conform it to specificities. One comes in the name of God and one in the name of the State. If this is internalized, death is very near. How can a vibrant, ever changing, and loving life accommodate one small person on one little planet somewhere in the deep recesses of space? Now this is an absurd notion!

Humanity is being showered with gifts, but it clings to scraps like a beggar. Many have attempted to stand between the people and God. The whole point of sharing spiritual information is to destroy the evil of the middleman and connect the individual with their own divine source. The aspirant often protects their pain much the way the completely unconscious does until they are clean and able to clearly reflect the Holy Spirit. From this place of liberation, the Zen Stick seems like a very compassionate instrument and the newly enlightened master thanks the Universe that there was someone heroic enough to overcome their poisonous vitriol and beat them over the head with the truth.

Ruminations of the Universe

Transcendence
Shed Your Insanity

However crazy the world seems, you can rest easy in knowing that you won't have to tolerate the situation forever. When you stand at the threshold of your own death it will seem to have gone by in a flash. All the fun and all the fury will dissolve in that single moment. The sum of your actions will come to a singularity. Those who have lived unconsciously serving Ego interests and trying to gain every scrap they can regardless of the effect they have on others will suddenly be hit with the hurt they have caused. Memories will flood in and tears will roll. Even when the body is lying in a heap, the soul will burn with the pain. This is hell.

If in this life you have consciously faced up to your karma and taken responsibility for the gift you have been given, you will slide over to the other side with continuity. There will certainly be some difficulties in the adjustment as very rarely someone skips over to the astral realms with glee, but over all there will not be an enormous pressure due to confrontation of the forgotten aspects of your being. It will not take long for you to create an environment of comfort and begin welcoming loved ones from the last life and all other lives to come in and visit you. If you enjoyed music on Earth you will still enjoy it in the astral. If you are an artist here, you will be one there.

When you agonize over the death of thousands of innocent people, take solace that you will soon follow. When you are angry at the political leaders making terrible decisions and trashing the planet, not to fear, they will quickly be in the dirt too. Watching television and smirking over the self-worshipping celebrities, don't be jealous, they will soon be bug candy. This hunk of flesh is temporary and we are just visiting here. It won't last long. Make love while you can; have a laugh while you can. Give your friend a hearty handshake and hug those you care about…every time. Say all that you have to say and don't hold back. Inhibition is due to believing the illusion.

Is it 2007, 2008, 2012, or 2209340982? Is it Monday, Friday, or Uhurbday? 3 o'clock, 9 o'clock or 171.00983 o'clock? Really it is none of these. The sun goes up…the sun goes down….the wheels keep on turning. If it rains, go outside and get wet. Run around like a maniac and when somebody looks at you stunned cry out, "Yes I am a loon, care to join me and shed your insanity?" If you like to go to the moon with your imagination, you are probably just remembering doing a few orbits in your dream state. This solar system is such a small place...just a neighborhood. Our little space probes are specs of what's possible.

We are overdue for populating the universe 'out there'. That is the only reason there seems to be too many people on Earth. Fighting with each other, we are slow to adapt technology. Do you really think there is enough 'gas' to get the heck out of here? Not a chance. New answers will be revealed to those who are ready. The greys will eventually leave us alone and the reptilian usurpers will be defeated like they have been every time they have tried to seize control. To understand them you will have to be schooled in the occult and metaphysical arts. They are indeed real, and you must be fully 'here' to deal with them. Beyond morality is another level of the struggle.

Transcendence
Skeletons Scare Minds

You could have died since the last chapter. Then you wouldn't give a shit about the TV news anymore. But oh well, let's pretend for a moment…..no let's not. Isn't that what is going so wrong? Pretending that things aren't so… It baffles me how people chop reality into pieces and then act like only a few of them exist.

You can swoop around and around the truth, coming to it in so many ways. Superimposing concepts on to what you see doesn't change it intrinsically. Truth remains as it is. It is you who are distorted. It is your mind coloring everything with clumps of conclusions. So many minds in closets of darkness… Maybe those skeletons will finally scare them out.

Driving forward, running from the past, we hope the arms of our precious future will take the pain away. Then one day we arrive at the location we prayed we'd come to and the ground starts sinking like quicksand. Halfway into the hole, you cry out, "I'll do anything, just give me another chance!" For some reason the dirt pukes you up, you wipe yourself off and try again.

Now, open and learn. Lo, ye who arrives. Fluidity in the present is the luxury we are missing. This is not some metaphysical hooey unless interpreted by a hooey head. I'm tired of messing around. Let's get the job done. (Someone offstage yells, "Over here! Over here!") Would you please tell them that you are going to Love yourself first this time?

If they come back, tell them that you have moved. It won't be a lie if you are alive. Sharing and empathy come after you can smile at the mirror. Feeling is just as important as thinking. Remind the men because sometimes they think they are too tough; someday we will look back and label them 'behind the times'. It is powerful and fulfilling to open your heart. Try it.

Transcendence
The Really Real

Guilt and fear are the real inflictors of terror. To invoke this in others is a true crime against humanity. Judgment is the ultimate weapon of mass destruction. Rather than destroying bodies, these poisons destroy souls. All natural flow freezes up and inhibition rules the day. Denial is the jailer and the poor people of the Earth become perpetual prisoners.

As time passes and these habits become more and more ingrained, the essence within is harder and harder to reach. Causing stress and arguments in place of relaxation and contentment, these foreign entities seek to perpetuate themselves through others. If confronted with the eye of awareness they will shriek and howl.

Zen masters of old would beat the demons out of their disciples. Eventually the disciples would be full of gratitude because they had no idea how bad things were and the master in his benevolence took it upon himself to reach past the corruption and make some space for the inner light to come in and begin to disperse the darkness. As the natural energies return to their true course, the heart opens and radiates Joy.

To find the infinite Source within, much diligence is needed. Instant reactions have to be replaced with the stillness of observation. Most people believe that they are the inculcated patterns of behavior and define themselves as such. If a friend comes along and suggests that perhaps it would be a wiser course of action to stop condemning oneself, the first response is often a "How dare you!?" audaciousness that tries to inflict the guilt and judgment directly on the friend.

With the true teachers of Tao, there is no one there to feel offended and the Will remains strong. Existence itself looks through their eyes and continues in a myriad of ways to plant seeds in the world for the magic awakening to take place. The walls are thick and defenses are constantly reinforced. Even if the entire outer world tells you that you are wrong, it may just be that you are right. Trust yourself and anything at all is possible. Beyond even the most extensive and fantastic dreams is the really real.

Transcendence
The Beast of Revelation

The Beast of Revelation is Mass Media. IT has come up from the pit and been loosed upon the world. In every home the Beast seeks to reside. Beyond rulers and countries, the living presence of The Beast is what essentially eats up people and then spits out their carcass for all to gape at before moving on to the next tasty morsel. Worshipped by the masses, the transitory images are simply the distraction which allows the Beast to feed upon the soul.

The Beast's favorite tricks are to tantalize with love-less sex, lies, violence, and emotional pain. 'Isn't it fascinating to watch people hurt?' IT is the opposite of peace. Let us not forget The Beast's propensity towards mixed messages, shaming people while perpetuating the very climate IT condemns. IT judges others who take life while justifying IT's own reasons for doing the same. IT bombards with so many graphic images that it scrambles the mind and undermines the individual's self-determination.

Beckoning you with your own secret desires, the Beast asks you to join the team. 'You will gain the world,' IT says with forked tongue and black heart. If you resist you will be an enemy. IT will not allow you to sit passively by; IT will force you to make a choice. It takes great inner fortitude and the willingness to make sacrifices for Integrity in order to keep a spiritual life going. The Beast has tried to co-opt that too. Every religion reduced to a system; every 'holy book' considered law.

A sure way to get the Beast's attention is to present an alternate message. Be they men or women, if they perpetuate IT's work they are anti-Christ. The anti-Christ(s) serve the Beast. They make sure to keep the ball rolling. They are hypnotized by the euphoria their limited power gives them. Controlling others, the food for the Beast passes through them and they are flushed with energy. They must keep this flow going in order to get their fix and keep the Beast from devouring them.

The devices of delivery for the Beast seem to be made by man but really man was serving the astral magnetism of the Beast. Coalescing ideas from the collective subconscious, the means for the message was willed into existence. Consider that there is no one person who makes up a network. A network forms organically. The Beast is really the suppression of humanity throughout history come to life to exact revenge for being banished from reality.

Transcendence

The only way to stop the Beast is to deflate IT's energy by accepting that which IT uses to hold us in fear. All individual pain must be transformed and the healing reverberations will echo throughout the Universe. With meditation and inner space we ascend to an untouchable place. With an Eye on the Beast and a Heart that's in Peace we reside in Heaven even if the World goes to Hell. All ancient myths are true; all realities exist simultaneously.

Ruminations of the Universe

Transcendence
The Conspiracy Religion

Beware my friends of one of the greatest consciousness traps out there today. Waking up to the fact that there are many specters across the globe that seek to enslave humanity, it is essential not to get fixated on this and allow it to possess your mind. What a joy it must be for the darkness to see that people fear every little thing, from cameras on the corner, to their cell phones eavesdropping on them, to King George sitting in his easy chair listening to you gossip about your plans for the holiday season.

Beyond all the details, they are invoking a state of mind. Some of you out there beginning the search for truth in a world gone mad will suddenly realize this superimposition of another layer of human reality that has been carefully crafted for thousands of years by various groups of secret societies. Now this is not so hard to believe once you get used to the idea. It is also not hard to imagine an extraterrestrial or demonic assistance to these nefarious forces once you break out of 5 sense perception and realize that there are many more activities going on just out of sight.

Breaking out of the hold of political persuasion and religious dogma we track down the criminals who have been perpetuating these lies to humanity's detriment and emphatically return responsibility to where it belongs. Those who do the difficult dirty work of bringing this information to the light of day are doing a great and courageous service, but the work does not end here. The point of knowing is to be free from influence, so that you can return to the beauty of life on Earth unencumbered.

If you are stuck pointing the finger of blame, then you are frozen in the reaction to the mind control which is simply mind control once removed and still serves the purpose of the legions of doom. The same is true for many of the people who 'fight for peace'. What if we were to take all of the masters of misery and throw them back in the pit they crawled out of? Do we have an alternative ready to go? It is the old story of revolution and what happens once you actually succeed.

Take care not to draw conclusions and make the story of conspiracy a dogma in its own right. Skull and Bones, the NWO, the Federal Reserve, crushing of human rights, etc… Yes, yes, yes, quite true. But so what? As a culture of humanity of course we have to remove this garbage from our path. At this point do you not get it yet? Does recounting it again and again help you? Does cowering in fear and despair help in our evolution to a spiritual species? The situation is far from hopeless.

Thinking about it and constantly reporting about it gives it existence in a more substantial way once you cross a certain threshold. It is a balance. We need to know the information, but once we do, we should not beat it into our brains or give it energy so that it is empowered by our attention. At this point we need to come back to the middle way and find a balance within our souls. Any story told too many times will become an obstacle to the real, because the real needs no fairy tale.

The essential point is that none of it exists in your inner world. There is you and life. Remove all the thorns and turn inwards. This is the heavenly purpose of the pain. Learn the lesson. It is not up to you to carry the weight of the world and the problems of all ages. It is up to you to do your part to awaken the spirit that the Universe endowed you with so that this divine spark can add to the chorus of voices changing darkness into light. The deepest truths are the same now as they ever were. There is no modernity in existence. It is all perfect as it is. We simply need to surrender the Ego to let God do the work of cleaning up this mess.

Ruminations of the Universe

Transcendence
Hotline to God

Don't look to others to determine if you are proceeding well on the path. There is no way anybody else can know the deepest part of you because this is precisely where your own unique divinity lies. Beware of adding more and more garbage to your cage by accumulating beliefs and knowledge. Pure truth is outside of the realm of the mind. This is an enormous threshold to overcome. Forces of darkness pump prepackaged thoughts straight into the minds of the masses through every means possible. TV, Radio, Signs, and most dangerously of all, once an individual is co-opted, they become an agent of the forces that have subverted their soul.

People gather around and support each other's illusions. Using the talking points that have been provided for them by media outlets, they feel good in being "informed". Imprisoning themselves in a bubble of deception, they think they are "secure". The more they are crushed, the safer they believe themselves to be. This is mainly because their reality has been turned inside out. After awhile they become so attached to being controlled and abused that they are terrified to leave. Anybody who comes to save them from this HELL ON EARTH will be seen as an enemy because their cherished systems must come crashing down for salvation to be possible.

You can dismantle this leviathan bit by bit, or you can leap out of the false perception of self by getting distance from the mind. I can guarantee to you that this is something that can be achieved. Most American's Minds have a stranglehold on them. To the rest of the world, consider this when you see madness raging this way and that. Americans are pumped full of propaganda, straight into this mind. They are told again and again that this is who they are. Since they do not know themselves because meditation, art, and music are almost nowhere to be found, they are susceptible and weak. They are trained early on in school to operate solely through the mind, as if that was all there is.

Many Americans are like shadows; empty bodies of habit bumping into each other and the world. There is no way an outsider can possibly know what it is like to be here. It is like a bad acid trip that never ends. All of the noble qualities in humanity are shunned. Such things as truth, integrity, trust, and love are discarded for empty belief, raw power, and gross self-indulgence. Most are far past the point of no return and will indeed careen right off the cliff with their demonic leaders. If you consider the phenomenon of 1000s of people that believe exactly the same thing, you will start to see more deeply into what is occurring. All whose hearts and minds have been corrupted essentially operate as a hive. Anybody not in the hive will be collectively shunned.

Those of you who still have heart, individuality, and the courage to carry on bless you. Know this control mechanism and stay true to yourself. Be a self contained unit of bliss. Life on Earth is still as beautiful and wondrous as it ever was if you can unplug yourself from the machine. Unravel all the crap and see life again for the first time. It is an intricate and unlikely series of events that provides you this opportunity for self discovery. Battles with your fellow human beings simply distract you from the essential cause. All the noise is on the surface. The depth of the ocean is where you'll find the mysteries. People and ideas come and go. Truth carries on throughout eternity. Take the time to connect with your own natural gifts and you will see that this is the hotline to God.

Transcendence
Earth Alliance with Grey Aliens

The Earth planet, also known as Gaia, Shan, Urantia, and Zion has been monitored for many thousands of years. The grey aliens are the most commonly accepted form of alien and many take it as a given that they are here and involved in human affairs. They crossbreed human and alien DNA to create a race that displays the best attributes of each. This entity will then be planted on another planet and given a chance to evolve. The grey aliens simultaneously have individuality and a telepathic mind in union with others. What they lack is inspiration and passion. If you have ever seen an image in popular culture with the grey aliens surfing or meditating, it is indicative of the human inclusion into their world. They seek to integrate this independence and freedom of spirit.

Very much like super scientists with very little feeling, the greys are currently beholding to their reptilian rulers who are located somewhere in the Orion belt. These reptilians contain among them some remnants of Dinosaur DNA harvested from Earth at an earlier time, just before the extinction event. They have long been interested in coming home and the greys are their information gatherers. Some reptilians have been living in secret corners of the Earth and some project psychically. They are both in the physical and astral planes and represent a certain aspect of nature's cold and cunning survival instinct. They are much more dangerous than the greys. The greys after exposure to humanity are starting to break away and discover life.

The greys followed WW2 very closely and when the US exploded the first nuke, humanity reached a milestone. Ever since there have been contacts between government and alien representatives. 1947 was an accident/incident that happened following early communications. There is an extensive network of tunnels inside the Earth that have markings from many different planets. Travel is quick and humanity at large barely notices the crafts that come and go. Occasionally a display is made where a large ship slowly passes over an area of the population. This is actually found to be the best way to keep people in the dark. Expose a small number of them to a phenomenon and leave the rest to speculate and attack each other. What is left is confusion.

Neither the greys nor the reptilians understand the ways of higher astral entities. They have managed to contact demons and inflict much pain, but have been held in check by angels and the energy fields of wisdom bearing humans.

Transcendence

There are groups on the planet that spend much time simply meditating; holding back darkness and bringing in light. The greys have access to technology that is far beyond the standard human fare, but that does not mean they understand the ways of the Tao. The reptilians are out of balance because they lack heart. Once they become a bit more awakened to potential in other directions maybe their actions will be more interesting than simply replaying the cycles of history.

There is a legend among the greys about the spirits who incarnate in human bodies. Translated most closely as:

Some will be habits.

Some will be smiles.

Some will be darkness.

Some will be bliss.

As humans the greys will become our students and we shall assist them in finding hope and they shall assist us in unshackling our species from the grip of the reptilians. Teach the greys the ways of Love and the psychic attacks of fear will lose power. The greys are very impressionable and lacking in Will they have been influenced by any who project outward with focus and intensity.

With our help they can become strong and more a part of our regular planetary life. Without the reptilian influence we can share technology and find peace. At this point as an alliance we can present ourselves to the rest of the Universe as ambassadors of good will in tune with the Creator.

Transcendence
Sacred Road of Freedom

Perhaps one day we will convene a meeting to discuss our successes and failures while on the Earth. There will be no judges, just lively conversation about the happenings encountered while incarnated in the body. No longer encumbered by the density of gravity, our ability to see clearly will pierce the illusions which often sway those on the ground disconnected from their soul. With chuckles and shrieks of horror we analyze and extract the lessons from the experience. The throbbing heart of the living Gaia makes it all possible and spirits from across the galaxy flock here to live her lucid dream.

With Christs, Krishnas, and Buddhas to forge a path, we have some reference to the sacred road of freedom. Dear people, realize that they would not want you to worship them, but to follow their example. How messages get distorted when told millions of times to millions of people for thousands of years! Strange as it may seem, often exactly the opposite of what is intended becomes the meaning attributed to the original sage's divinely inspired messages. These truths do not come from the clouds, but are already written deep within all of our hearts. We are constantly told to look outside; nay, look in.

What we normally think of as life on Earth is merely the absolute surface of what is possible to comprehend. The dangers of constant entertainment are that you become occupied for every second of your waking life to the neglect of the extensive inner world just waiting to be awakened and cultivated. Every bit of light you shine inwards changes what is possible outside. Strength, courage, and determination will help you to find what it is you seek. There is no chance of failure if you keep going. Only if you give in to the pressures and demands of worldly ways will you lose the precious jewel of your soul.

Once you have come to know the character of your spirit, there is nothing that can ever take it from you. No matter what you come across, you will be able to negotiate the circumstance with dexterity and the fragrance of your grace will leave blessings in its wake. Flowers bloom in the aura of the enlightened one. If you are lucky enough to find a being with these heavenly qualities, drop everything and go to them. Try not to bombard them with trivialities. Instead sit with them, and turn your whole energy to soaking up their vibe. Drink deeply of this profundity and you will find that within you is the same.

Transcendence
A Better World for All of Us

One day soon, you'll wake up to see that things have changed. They always do change, but we get lulled to sleep with repetition. Even those circumstances we thought we could count on sometimes reveal themselves to be less than solid. The more we hold our attachments, the more will be the pain when they are taken away. This pain is not to punish us, but to reorganize our priorities from temporary possessiveness to eternal awareness. Don't take anything for granted and don't expect that what you have today will be there tomorrow. Be ready to walk away before you bow your head and you will be master of your own dominion.

If you are absolutely certain of the correctness of your own position, take heed. A wise person is open to many different possibilities. Even a casual passerby can sometimes act as the universe in disguise and slip you a gem if you are ready to hear it. Once you start chopping existence into pieces you've destroyed the synergy which displays its ultimate life force. Let mind rest and feel the breeze. Gaze at the beauty of the garden without interpretation. Be grateful for what you have; this will attract even more joy and abundance.

There are conspiracies aplenty, ghosts, aliens, demons, and all types of conscious entities both visible and invisible. Until we are settled in our own center of power, many of these things can do us more harm than good. Wait until you've deprogrammed your mind, healed your emotions, and gotten over yourself to dabble deeply in the more active esoteric side of spiritual discovery. Some think the goal is to lay bare every tidbit to any novice and let them run wild. Do we give a baby a knife? Busting loose Kundalini in one who is not ready can mess them up for life.

Many who are confused after ingesting heavy amounts of psychedelics such as LSD or mushrooms are suffering from having seen too much too soon. They can often be helped back from the edge by explaining it in these terms. Meditation brings you to the places of which drugs can only give you a passing glimpse. Indeed those trees are pulsing and the colors in the sky are a tremendous tapestry of divine art. With clarity beyond judgment that reflects what is, we live every moment with this intensity and brilliance. There is a vibrant reality just out of sight that is far more extensive than the one we can see with our outer eyes.

Transcendence

There is little in this life more valuable than trust. Words are extremely significant and should not be thrown about unconsciously. Among the earliest and most powerful forms of magic, we are casting spells every time we speak. More so, even when we think, we are bringing resonant energies into play. What's on your mind tends to shape your world. This is why surrounding yourself with good influences is important as they tend to uplift your general mindset, creating a better life for you and making a better world for all of us.

Ruminations of the Universe

Transcendence
A New Beginning

It is not surprising that the 4th Reich would be even more dramatic and short lived than the 3rd. This time the people turned back tyranny not with guns, but with information and heart. The light invasion did indeed defeat the evil winds. As suddenly as they disappear they can reappear. Do not be caught napping as these trends never wholly evaporate. They cyclically come to darken humanity's day, so we must be ever vigilant so that the controllers never get back to power.

NeoCons are the Nazi's of the 21st Century. Devaluing life, they spread fear to get the masses to submit to control. Conjuring enemies they seek a perpetual state of war so as to provide justification for the usurping of human rights. Whatever happened on 9/11, it was certainly used as cover for one of the most horrible shifts in political thinking to have ever occurred. It is a wonder in this modern age of miracles that we can not do better at solving the world's problems. Nationalism itself keeps solutions from being rendered. There is one Earth and many splendid creatures upon it.

This may be an end of sorts, but the new beginning is of even greater consequence.

Democrats may well be the less awful of our choices for now, but that does not mean we do not continue to progress. Kick the Democrat's rears to actually back up the rhetoric on health care and education (including funding for art, music, health [sex], philosophy, psychology, and information technology.) Every place you see remnants of the destructive NeoCon mindset, continue to confront it with deeper and more profound truths. There really isn't much to celebrate yet. In fact an honest response would be mourning and quick work to rectify.

Republicans might want to 'put the election behind them', but it isn't that easy. Aren't they famous for howling about accountability? The whole Neo-Con era should be investigated thoroughly and all pathways followed to their ultimate conclusion. A De-NeoCon-ification should be made standard for those who were caught up in the madness. Let's open government up from its secrecy, and take a more enlightened approach when communicating with the populace. We can become the beacon of hope the world longs for us to be.

Deep bonds of friendship and equality should be established between a free US and the European Union. How can we dictate to the land which gave us birth? More and more we should work together to create wise policy. A North American Union isn't necessarily bad if it is not in exploitive hands. It would make exchange of resources flow more easily. There truly are no borders in the Universe. What we see are stages of development. Eventually all nations will unite and be no more separate. We will remember them all as flavors of the world stew.

We must begin to turn back the aggression on the planet. Pulling out of Iraq will not create any more disaster than what is already there. Of course there will be an adjustment period that is fairly chaotic. They were just invaded, had their leader abducted, and thousands of their people mowed down! If they can get electricity and water they are lucky, let alone set up the halls of democracy. Perhaps they are wondering whether their voice will ever be heard within the imposing walls of W.'s new Baghdad palace. This immense military base is built over one of the portals to the underground empire.

No further military aggression should be tolerated. World peace will not be found until Israel's incursions are halted as well. If they attack Iran unilaterally, the United States should turn away. The Israeli's are not God's chosen people. Each human has a divine birthright. We all must transform the sins of the past to heal the present. The Native American injustice, the slave trade, the rape of the land full of wolves, bear and buffalo, the civil war, the atrocities of WW1, 2, and 3, to all battlefields throughout history, we must recognize the whole of reality and make a fundamental change.

It may take some time but eventually the realization of what happened in America will sink in. The implications are profound and far-reaching. Chemical and psychological experiments have been enacted on a whole nation of people. The treasure of our country has been plundered through war contracts and rebuilding corporations. We have become accustomed to inept leaders who spy on us and lie without flinching. To this day they show no hint of remorse. Thankfully there are signs that people are finally turning away from this mental illness. Let's take some time to clear the mind. Then we can relax and open our hearts.

Transcendence
Transcend the Circumstance

Speaking on behalf of individual independence and self-determination free from intimidation, bombardment, and subconscious coercion is speaking for the heart of the true American vision. Dreams are too surreal and unnecessary when clear ideas can be manifested and quickly implemented to solve the real problems on the ground.

Can we scarcely imagine what could be done if even half of the money spent in war was spread around in science and the arts. We could be growing as people and prospering as a nation. There is absolutely no reason not too. There is no such thing as 'time' and 'history'... they are the echoes of the old world haunting our present. With courage and clarity we should together move on.

Divide and conquer is the oldest enemy of the human race. It begets a chain reaction that eventually knocks on every door. When one occurrence finally calms down there are already several more on the way…and this goes on in perpetuity. The way to stop the cycle is to identify the situation and transcend the circumstance. Hold this bit of wisdom close to your heart, for it is the key to illumination.

Do you ever wonder what kinds of secrets the occult wizards of the world hold? How about the magic deep inside the Vatican library? Would you like to know about cultures before the Egyptians such as the Atlantians, Lemurians, and the Vedic Indians? Or know more about space visitors, other dimensions, and psychic powers? Then my friend I say it again, transcend the circumstance.

Do not let your few life events define who you are and the positions you hold. Get up and out of yourself and look at the world from the sky. So many tiny people with thousands of little squabbles are all bustling about. You could blow a puff of air and make it all go away.

Come to know your body and how it works as if it was some kind of alien technology with sight, sound, taste, touch, and smelling capabilities…an Earth space suit that gathers data and makes constant imprints in the brain. One day the dreamer will awake and find that what they thought was life was death and what they feared the most was life.

All spectrums go on past our external perceptive capabilities, but when we sink our awareness back into the astral body, we can perceive everything at once. When we go beyond the

Transcendence

concept of time, not only this time-line, but all potential time-lines converge as a singularity. This is where you become a 5th dimensional being.

At oneness, feel the entire continuum of the 4th dimensional astral realm, and reside completely in the moment in the physical body on 3rd dimensional Earth. Sliding in between realms there is nothing conceivably off limits or impossible. There are still random variables and the works of others happening. There is a certain order and an arena.

Whatever you find most amazing about the universe will reveal itself more and more. Letting yourself merge with the whole by dissolving Ego you begin to hear about everything that has ever happened on every level. There is drama, humor, ache, and joy; music, swirling colors, beautiful patterns, and a tremendous sense of fulfillment.

Every friend you've ever had is here. Nothing can be lost. It all works out in the end. Thank you so much for any kind thought you have ever given me. If anything I have ever done has touched you, let me say it has been my honor. To serve our true nature is a far greater gift than anything else in the world.

Ruminations of the Universe

Enlightenment 2

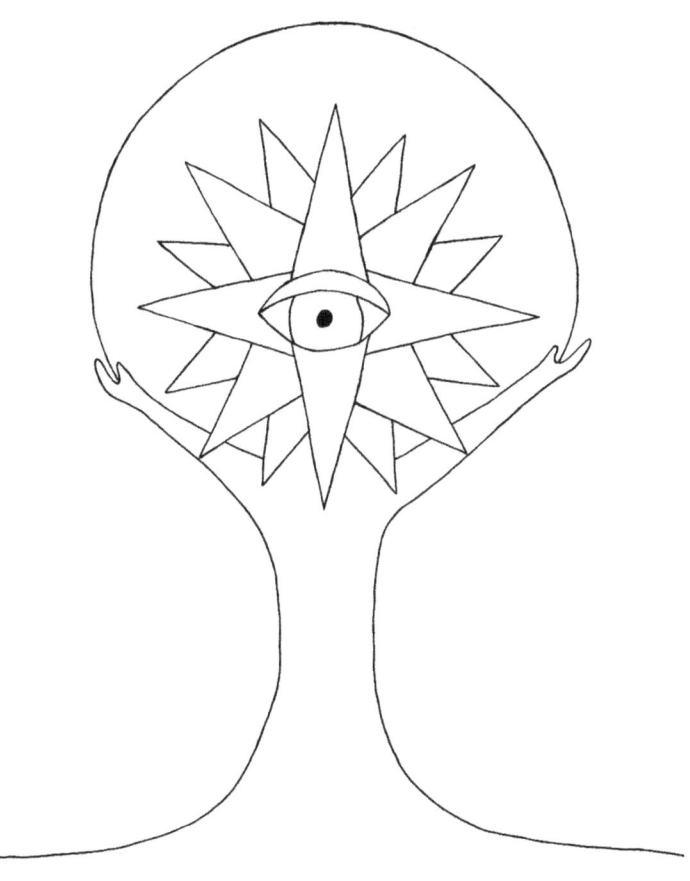

Enlightenment 2
Magical Buddha Nature

The Tao is not obliged to follow any expectations of the one attempting to align with it. There may be disparate lessons to learn and once the seeker has made an inner pledge to put enlightenment before the ways of the world, the Universe will begin to provide the scenarios for you to fulfill your mission. This may mean that you will have to move again and again. New cities, new relationships, and plenty of uncertainty await the adventurous spirit. The master of the moment will meet you exactly where you need and the ecstasy is in direct correlation to the ability to risk.

There is a Zen saying that stands in contrast to what many in the West consider wise counsel: "Don't look before you leap!" If everything is premeditated we can transfer the safety of our personal parameters to the future so that we never have the naked brilliance of a truly new experience. This way we might be able to temper fear, but we also live at the minimum and have no room for the divine to enter our hearts. Love is above all things the freedom of expansion. If this is not what you feel, all the rationalizations in the world will not change the situation. Only a leap will.

Can you tell what it is your heart is saying to you? There will be many voices crowding your inner world with very serious and authoritarian structures that seem to make much sense. "You got to do this…you got to do that….its a rough world out there…" Shab once said something quite simple to me that has many implications. "Either the Universe is a magical place or it isn't." Huh? Well, if it isn't, then it is a cold, dark and lonely place and we are pretty much helpless. If it is, Love is possible, dreams can be realized, and we can work with the magic to create our own joy.

In this accelerated way of life, letting go is the key ingredient. It is possession which makes us scream with pain. When it is time for change and we resist, it hurts. The more we drag our heels, the more excruciating it will be. As much as we may Love something or someone, there will come a time when we go it alone. If we can find comfort in this place then all that we do have can be enjoyed to a greater extant than if we were attempting to live in a manner worshipping accumulation. This is why money can never make us happy; it does nothing to fill the inner void.

The heart has its own methods. If you give you will get more. If you hold back, the little you do have will dry up like a tiny sprout in the desert sun. Consider experience and enjoyment your guides to success. You didn't go through the whole incarnation trauma to sit in front of your TV sets all day every day. Nor did you take that initial plunge to just punch the old time clock in your work-a-day world. You did it to find the truth of who you are. There may be layers of dust upon your soul, but a fresh wind can clear the mirror and with just a peak you will see your Buddha nature.

Ruminations of the Universe

Enlightenment 2
Tao has a Way

Following the heart and not the head is at once a rewarding and harrowing experience. As you ease off the Ego and learn to trust intuition, life can begin to take you to your greater destiny. Many make their decisions based on mental rationalizations derived from various external sources. Calculations designed to reach personal ambitions lead the individual to build walls and fight reality for momentary gain. Worldly acclaim builds the Ego up and pride takes over rendering the spirit inaccessible. Decorating the self with temporary treasures, death sneaks up and takes it all away. In the last few seconds of Earthly existence the person realizes the terrible mistake they have made, but alas it is too late.

Changing from the narrowing effect of mental desires to the expansion of inner truth is a significant moment in any person's journey. The most important thing to facilitate the process is the ability to admit that following the values of the world does not bring lasting fulfillment. No matter how many ribbons and certificates of achievement, unless you release your inherent nature, you will still be discontent. It is difficult to take this step because there is much pressure from the outside for you to continue to tow the party line. If you go your own way it will be a disruption for the status quo. They will think you have suddenly gone crazy; now you are a stranger among them. Even those you love may subtly pressure you. There is much momentum to the same old story.

In the world, 'A' leads to 'B' which leads to 'C' which leads to 'D'. In spirit, 'A' could be followed by 'Z' to swing around to 'N' on the way to 'F'. The 'ABC'ers' will certainly think it mad to leap hither and thither, but as Osho has said many times, heart has its own logic. Charting a standard course according to mind, you limit the energies available to you. Rejuvenation may only be available if you break the old patterns and move to the utterly new. There are so many people to meet and options to explore; it is a shame if you spend life going in circles. One never knows what the 'morrow will bring. This is part of the beauty and adventure of being here. So many times if you allow and let change, life will bring you what you didn't even know you needed.

Every thing that happens is designed to teach you life lessons. Nothing occurs in happenstance. In any given situation you will be stagnant until you get the point of it and proceed to the next scenario. Once you get used to living in this way

Enlightenment 2

you move more freely and doubt your inclinations less and less. With no expectations, there are no disappointments. Past disappears as soon as it is over and future is created in the present. With awareness, humor, and courage the fear of the unknown is conquered and the higher energies of life are released. The joy of following the heart's path starts spreading to those around you. Soon, your light and happiness becomes contagious and others start stirring from their slumber. Indeed, Tao has a way.

Ruminations of the Universe

Enlightenment 2
Treasure Your Divinity

A grand bridging of systems occurs when you correlate dimensions and the actual heavenly bodies around us. We have often heard about becoming one with all things, and that we are bringing light to humanity. To clear that matter up, we simply turn to Our Father who Art in Heaven, the Sun. Sol's heat, warmth, and radiance not only sustain life on the outside, but there is a more direct connection on the inside.

As long as we are looking outward there is 3D and more 3D universe, because we perceive only with the sense instruments of the body which exists in the physical world. When we meditate we withdraw our attention from these devices and let our energy start moving in another direction. This experience is something most people have never had so they will need patience in order to learn to recognize it. It is not difficult, only a matter of whether or not the individual will bother to take the time.

As we learn to value meditation, and are no longer constantly occupied by the outside cacophony or the mind which brings it to you, we can sink into our astral body which exists in the astral realms or the 4th dimension. This is not just one single frequency but a range within a continuum of vibration. Even while your physical body lives in the physical, the astral body simultaneously lives in the more fluid astral universe. Withdrawing from the surface you see that the world within is infinitely more vast than the world without, which you previously thought was all that existed. Your astral body has a visual capacity from the aura, the ability to tune in telepathically to many types of entities, the talent to hear celestial music, and the skill to digest large amounts of information almost instantly.

This astral body is made up of 7 major chakras correlating with 7 colors of the Earth rainbow, many smaller chakras, and the aura or energy skin of the light being. This body exists within the Earth's radiant sphere which gives rise to the 4th dimension. The Earth has a physical body, which we can walk about on, and also a soul within this spherical body that gives birth to nature, and interacts with the Sun so as to make Life here possible. We continue in our progression from bodies to spheres to stars. This is where the cycles of soul incarnation meet up with those who are on Earth. It is well known amongst many that Souls born on the Earth world work their way up from the dirt. From stones to plants, to animals, to man, with of course many further variations along the way. Earth is doing

Enlightenment 2

the great painful creative work of contributing original souls to the galaxy.

Many more souls on Earth just swooped in from other places, grabbed a body and started having experience. Many underestimated the denseness of Earth's gravity. This is part of the effect She has on beings who come near. If they have the capacity for heart, it might well become awakened, if they have the sensibility for feeling, they may learn to understand the subtleties of its grace. Gravity and the magnetic field of the Earth are physical indicators of the realms that are born in the higher vibrations around her. Many souls literally orbit the Earth reincarnating again and again until gaining enough self awareness that they can lift back off and carry on the journey.

Beings coming in from other parts of the galaxy have an easier time mastering the Earth way. Buddha was a space traveler who brought ancient wisdom from many other cycles of incarnation on many other planets in many other star systems. His calmness and clarity helped bring peace and order to many on the planet. It is no wonder many view him as a god because in a way He is as is any who come to such depth where they speak as Existence itself. He was able to escape the Solar System.

Many who begin to walk the way or get into new age materials get captivated at the first hints of the astral world. Ghosts, demons, angels, and many more entities are suddenly all around when you become aware of your astral body. They always were, and most likely were always interacting with you before, you just weren't consciously aware of it. The initial stages can be confusing because you can perceive such a wide range of phenomenon. With no reference point in the mind and without the validation of your fellow man, you might begin to doubt your own sanity until you find a teacher who understands or consciousness related materials you resonate with. Some are so enamored that they never escape this place, believing the closest astral realms are all of heaven. Not so. It is just the very beginning; the closest vibration to ours and the first layer of reality beyond our own. Many on Earth are here to become immersed in the experience so as to open their heart. This is graduation from Earth Academy.

To truly open the heart and manage this enormous realm within us while still keeping watchful meditative space, one needs the awareness that comes from returning to the Source. For most of us here that will be our friend Sol or as many call Him, the Sun. We described the astral body as the color spectrum of chakras. As with any spectrum it springs from a singularity, or the white light. This white light is the light of the Sun. This is where we meet as one. When we are free from the ties that bind, we can unify and know the mind of Sol with all its Secrets of the Solar System. Further, from this point you can communicate to other stars and hear the ruminations of the entire Universe. The monk has now integrated the Heart (Earth, Mother), and become One with the Father (Sun).

As previously mentioned, some of us came to this solar system from elsewhere. If we are ever going anywhere but here we are going to have to lift out of even the 5D communion with the Sun and be free of all attachments to everything that happened while in all bodies 3D-5D. Most of us have spent significant time on the Earth, and some of us even visited Minerva (the asteroid planet), Mars, and various moons. Will we ever forget drifting around the rings of Saturn or playing near the warmth and power of Jupiter's musical embrace? What a marvelous time it has been here! Yes there is much tumult on the surface of Earth's world, but it is all designed to get you to look inwards so you can find the treasure of your divinity.

Ruminations of the Universe

Enlightenment 2
Transcendent River

Many times the wisest of sages refer to the Tao as being like a river. This is as close to an approximation as possible using human language and mental references. Things are always changing. There is no point where anything is at a standstill. We are sometimes lulled into believing that they are because of slow vibration and the Earthly passage of time. Allow scientific principles to become a type of vision in your method of reckoning. If you look hard enough you will be able to see that the table you thought was solid is really a multitude of atoms endlessly buzzing. Manifested items are really quite temporary. They might hold pattern integrity for 10, 50, or even 100 years or more, but what is that in the belly of infinity? Each creation is like a dream that comes and goes rather quickly.

How much do we have to unravel to understand with our own being, the nature of the Universe? All the way, because any imprint left will color that which IS. Starting with where you are this moment, go backwards through this lifetime you have been living. Strip off the layer of social conditioning, schooling, family values, and fundamental divisions in your mind. Allow yourself to reflect the whole of reality at once.

The process of deprogramming one life is somewhat known, but if you truly seek to fully recover cognizance of your highest self, you will have to unravel the mess of your past lives as well. There are all kinds of Karmic threads we must end; also much experience we can benefit from to be assimilated. Hold awareness and allow your truth to unfold without doubt.

Again we dive into our brain at the level of the synapse. Even as you and I might discuss something, so too does one synapse fire some information to another. Now imagine a room full of people/synapses all shouting to be heard. Sound like any Mind you might know? Which voice should we choose to listen to? Actually none of them are the correct one. Synapses all reflect some external stimulus until you gain the understanding that grants them the freedom of rest and silence at long last. In meditation we often hear that the seeker is to become silent. This may feel like oppression at first because most only know silence as a forced thing. When we release our attention from identification with the crowd's chatter, we effortlessly relax in a pool of healing energies. Here we hear our heart.

Buddha uses the method of negation to reveal transcendent reality. The peculiar nature of the situation is such that if he were to suggest to you something in the positive, it would become the very obstacle which would keep you from seeing the same. Instead he says, *"No longer be distracted by the temporary oscillations of this and that. Forget petty concerns and value the opportunity. There is one reason we are here and I will remind you of it. I will not give you the answer. I will help you to discontinue hindering yourself. Stop and see."* We create the murky waters. If we let them settle, we will see to the bottom. We are connected to everything and what we witness outside is but the symbol of the deeper inner meaning. This is the secret that has been elusive to humanity.

Ruminations of the Universe

Enlightenment 2
The Kingdom is Yours

Don't wait for any government to collapse to get on with the process of discovering the ultimate truth. Historically these things can drag out for many years. Dec. 21, 2012 will be a good day for those who collectively understand certain realities to conceptually move ahead. For those of you waiting for Quetzalcoatl's Ghost to appear and rub the finger of shame at all evil doers, you might be waiting for a long time. There is not going to be anything like that because the actual shift in energy is deeper and more profound. The alchemy of transformation occurs through compression and release. Denial is the great deceiver and Ego is the gatekeeper.

There is nothing preventing you from doing anything you might want to do right now. The magic and wonder available with just a little meditation puts the whole of existence right at your mind's eye. Can you be bold enough to paint the canvas of your life? Make sure it isn't a psychological spew. Face the pain, cry a few tears and open your mind to new possibilities. Please watch out for premature conclusions. I know many people will read this and have an inbuilt assumption that they already understand all of what I am saying. Others might be highly critical and are certain that they can discount the points I make. Still more will grant the words favor and feel prideful because of it.

The great service I provide for you my friends is that you cannot pin me down with expectations. One time I might give a glimpse into the astral realms. Another, I will throw out a thousand ways to deconstruct the mind. I practically beg you to consider meditation and devote myself to providing any seeking soul with resources to explore. There is a science to spirituality and it is not one of black and white facts. It is based on personal experience and documentation. Many people are right now contributing to this growing and critically necessary body of literature. If you enjoy or benefit from this movement towards awareness, support these people when you find them. Give them respect in the light of day. Tell the world that you value substantive conversation. Share your own perspective.

There is a much bigger world out there than what we were taught in high school and college textbooks. Reality is amorphous and evolving, not rigid and absolute. There are as many versions of events as there are witnesses. We can not really say that anything is necessarily so. This is a philosophical question to zoom in on. Often the mind proves itself correct when dealing with the 3D realm. In 3D, a concept could seem correct, but one must not be so naive as to believe there is nothing beyond their local time and place. There are much bigger principles in play and when not viewing yourself as the focal point of life, you are free to receive the benefit that this understanding provides. It does not make sense to exclude the entire universe of possibilities to be "correct".

Hold on to your old religions. Grasp tightly to the legacy of your forefathers and three mothers. Cling to the covers of dusty books. Dance around and display this marvelous knowledge to passersby. Just know one thing: do so at your own peril. You could force a person to stop mentioning this point, but it would not change a thing about the implications that only a friend attempts to reveal. This Earthly life is very cause and effect oriented. So often people mistakenly believe that effects just happen to them! Look over here from a star and you will see what I mean. Becoming fixated with the circumstances of incarnation, a person becomes a historical footnote before they even begin. Judging everything with a pre-programmed philosophy, all choices are skewed. Eventually every intention sent to the universe under this and any other spell has to be accounted for.

Those who praise your every move to high heaven are more dangerous than those who tear you down. We all seek to move from a destroyer, but a seducer can draw in even the best of us with a subtle web of lies. Always remember that you and only you can know the proper direction for the progression of your soul. A friend will encourage you and offer support. They will share their experience and accept you for who you are. An enemy will constantly undermine your confidence and present more practical alternatives to your dreams. The fulfillment you seek, only you can provide. This blossoming of existence will occur when you can be in tune with the heart in an unafraid and powerful manner. No one else controls your destiny. Trust and ye shall be rewarded. The entire kingdom is rightfully yours.

Enlightenment 2
I Am You

The 'I' that I am and the 'I' that you are, are one and the same. It is consciousness itself that looks through both sets of eyes. We assume that our sense of self-awareness applies only to ourselves while others also do the same. All 'selfs' and the corresponding feelings/perceptions are processed simultaneously at the point of singularity transcendent to the shifting tides of time. If you become a mirror and I become a mirror, we will find that we are the same mirror. Our collective 'reality' is the phenomenon that is reflected passing through.

If you can consciously reside at the mirror point, then at any time you can become the mirror in the other, literally seeing for yourself through another's eyes. If you look deeply enough into any eye you will see that it is you looking at you. This can be found in a friend, a lover, or even in a favorite pet. After all, at the point of no division, life is life and its expressions are all demonstrative of the Creator's imagination. In each of our incarnated bodies, we reflect a series of happenings and the resulting expansion of understanding is sent back into the whole.

Being one with life, you are now able to see things from every perspective. Being every creature, you can no longer tolerate the cruelty that is inflicted upon nature with its myriad of justifications. Being the Earth, you know that to be cut deeply and bled dry is the reason for ferocious weather screams. Being the Sun, you understand that solar flares are indicative of the increase in energy being sent so as to awaken humanity before they destroy themselves. Being the Stars, you are beyond limitation and are absolutely certain that nothing is ever lost.

The Sun's son (or daughter) is awareness in us. We all come from the same Source. Swimming back upstream like the salmon through deprogramming the mind and healing the emotions, we make room for a deeper universal understanding. As soon as we interpret we will get confused. As long as we reflect, there is no limit to what we can ascertain. Watch everything and all will be revealed. The truth of life is very simple. We have made our world very complex. Stepping out of the body/mind shell we leave the madness behind.

Enlightenment 2
Inner Space

Let me share with you one of the trickier aspects of deprogramming. Someone who had hardship and a lack of unconditional love in their youth most likely will search for another way to live than how they were raised. Another who had things pretty well off and had many people around them who were generally kind may not see that there is something else to find. Good, bad, or any increment at all, if it is an impression in the mind that filters your experience, you are missing many layers of perception.

Systems of thought are not to be identified with. They are merely tools with which to sharpen your awareness. There is no need to choose one when you can expose yourself to all and be ready for the moment 'now'. Life is not about reacting. It is about acting in accordance with your inner Will and nature. The uniqueness of you is something no-one else can know. Just believe in yourself and heal the split caused by expectations from the outside. Release the guilt and allow the happiness that comes from fearlessly living the truth.

Try not to take provocations personally. That is how seekers again and again get mixed up. If you come to a master, you had better be prepared. The fastest way to transform into the next dimension is to allow some advice from someone who has gone on before. Then you can help the next young monk who comes along. Each time it gets quicker and easier because we support each other through the process and thoroughly document what we find along the way. There is much to share and no other way to prove it to the 'Normals'. Sleepwalking through life like shadows upon a distant memory they are but an echo of their full potential.

Who knows if we will wake up tomorrow? Create as if each day is the last. Leaving nothing unsaid, appreciate friends and give everything you have to give. This is not a choice to make, but a result of removing personal desire. How is this possible? By removing the 'self' that has the desire. There will definitely be a process left and a soul there to enjoy being incarnate; there will no longer be a rigid density that comes from believing in only one small set of pathways in one miniature mind. Things used to be this way, but spirit is more and more readily available. Many people claim they want the truth but will they receive it when it comes? Enlightenment happens over time for people only because it is too much to bear all at once.

Enlightenment 2

Allow your heart to open and move with the pathways of least resistance. Shake your head and see anew every moment of every day. What is right in front of you? Many gaze at the horizon while the answers they seek come to them in the form of synchronicities. Not noticing the clues, they have yet to discover the language of magic and the capabilities of the living dreamer. Looking towards tomorrow we often miss today. In the end, there is no other day. Many of us wish for a day when there will be more justice, yet compromise when we have the opportunity to demonstrate what is so needed in this world. It is you who are reading this and those people around you who are the awakening and the restoration of human dignity. There is no such thing as divisions on our world. Imagine what Earth would look like from a spacecraft in outer space. There is a globe with many humans and animals on it. Indeed it would seem perplexing all the butchery that is witnessed, but there would certainly be no lines as on a map and in our minds.

It is time to not hide from the ultimate reality. Let yourselves flow into the stream of energy that comes from the Source. You can still do all the things you ever did before. You will only enjoy them all the more. Setting free your innate talents, you will bloom like a flower and your fragrance will be released into the air. My version of this will be to have all of my creative work injected into the world wide web upon my death. Then I will forever be a part of the human program. Reflecting on these images, melodies, and words, the course of humanity will be forever altered. Each one of us makes a difference in the destiny of all. What are you contributing? Have you made the situation in the world better? Have you made one life better? These are not questions to be asked in judgment, but to provoke growth and the better parts of our soul. Too often when one thing is said, another is assumed. Try not to color this because there is much available if looked at absolutely clearly. Usually it is good to just move on; there will be a few of you out there compelled to look this communication over once more and in this case it will be beneficial. It is not a personal message but a transmission from soul to soul. There is a vibration song that beckons you to dance. There is an inevitability of success for those of you who lead with the heart and have the courage to do what you are born to do.

Enlightenment 2
The Universe is Looking for You

The Universe is looking for you. Sometimes it says hello in a bird's song or expresses love in another's embrace. Each life experience brings you closer to being completely open and available for the forces of creativity to flood into your body and awaken the slumbering spirit. Seeing everything with clear eyes, the moment is stark and brilliant. Things will be different now. Never again will you take the everyday miracles for granted.

There are countless tremendous happenings going on all around us. Change comes knocking at the door on a regular basis. You could stop and lock yourself into place, but one day you will have to suffer your rebirth. When you do, you will again see the hope and joy that resides within your heart. Let this explode to the world and you will create an oasis of bliss for wandering souls. Rest awhile and when you are ready, bravely face the unknown.

Undo imprints and let intuition sort out the rest. Trace everything back to its source and what is left will be light. Shine brightly and follow your inclination to its full fruition. Express everything and you will come to know who you are. Fear mongers may scowl at the real; simply know that it is your truth. Influence is unnecessary as every last detail may be found within. Circuitous routes seem to be the only roads that have the stones of full revelation.

When that which you thought was so becomes unraveled do not be scared. Embrace the exhilaration of exaltation released by a leap of faith. Diving to the bottom of the sea, we pull weeds and plant seeds. Remember that time is just a game with a good name. Smile knowing that you transcend all limitations and attempts at definition. People are processes and that which they seek is hiding in plain sight. In just a little while we can have it all.

Enlightenment 2
All Will Be Revealed

Enter the space of presence. Phase in to life. Relax enough to allow something new. Let go of that which is past its time. There are but a few moments between now and then. No simple solutions for the absence of problems. Look and walk; talk when ready. Dance on your tiptoes through the land mines. Giggle when you get a break. Fly with your astral wings and gravity is bound to come along. Those bad things you did only matter as much as they matter to you. People and Nature forget the wrongs after awhile. Celebrate the rights and let the rain cleanse you.

Heal wounds in the simple pleasantness of life consciousness. The greatest gift has already been given. We can make what we would like with it. Aspirations are one thing and creation is another. It is enough to enjoy. If you are happy you will help. Unbelievably serene and perfect in its synchronicity, the unfolding of the universal plan will inevitably bring everything exactly where it needs to be. This relieves much of the burden from our shoulders. Faith is much deeper than belief; it is inner conviction developed through observation and intuition that the cosmos has a plan.

Shining stars each and every one of you, smile at how far you've come. Remember when you were just getting ready to jump into the time portal that links the astral realm to the 3D world? Remember how before that you were extensively prepared to live the life you laid out for yourself? Back to the jungle you went with map in hand and the will to survive. How is it going? Don't believe the dense wave forms to be anything other than an aspect of terra firma. Stay far away inside when moving amongst the struggling crowds. When you Love, give totally and receive well.

Become your own Prince or Princess of Peace. It takes great power to keep the sword in the sheath. This is done with understanding, not suppression. Anything held under by force will one day take revenge. Balancing all the chakras, we find harmony in our being. Only then will be able to sort out the simultaneous messages we are receiving throughout the spectrum band. At any point, you may tune in to any frequency. You want to connect to Beethoven?....ZAP....how about your spirit guide?....ZAP....how about your dead grandfather?....ZAP.

We can go even further until we are diving deep into the source. There is no longer any need to hold things in your brain as it becomes an instrument in the service of AUM the all encompassing living vibration. It is like a million roller coasters of love and intelligence when invigorated with the Holy Spirit. Hello on behalf of the Universe; the closest one can come to speaking with Existence itself. This too is in you. Link to it and all will be revealed. Repeat: Link to it and all will be revealed. Repeat: Link to it and all will be…..

Ruminations of the Universe

Enlightenment 2
Space Gamblers Sip Pain and Pleasure Soup

Deep lethargy will envelope ye who stays the same. Complacency becomes your middle name and your life is lost in the game. Oft projected frequencies hiss with a static that reminds you of the word garbled. Feeling dizzy you rest for a moment, but the mind keeps on whizzing. Worried about tomorrow you fail to take care of today. Burdened with yesterday your present is a memory before it begins.

Doing a thousand things but none of them are quite right. It is better to clean the house and sit for a spell. Maybe in time the road will be smoother. Universality and the world need bridges that people can walk across. The span is vast and the arenas are moving farther apart. Only if we coax them together with song and celebration will many begin to arrive. Arm in arm we dance our way to the next moment of our lives.

There is a hill up ahead and I hear that behind it is a valley. People in this place whisper about things like Love, Death, Sex, and Enlightenment. Pain and pleasure are the flavors of the soup. Sometimes it is nice to add a little spice. How can it be that things pass away and leave us deserted? It must be a longer term plan to develop our finest inner sensibilities. Nobody can help us in this crushing and transformative process.

We are all gamblers or else we would not have come here. This is a wild and wondrous planet where anything can happen. Things can veer completely out of control. Even with best efforts, failure is quite possible and there are a lot of crazy variables. It is no surprise that humans like to build cages and hide in there. It is a modern version of bunkering in caves while dinosaurs thunder across the countryside.

Dependency is like a drug. It saps you of strength and dignity. Independence has to be claimed. In order to leave this Earth with integrity intact, one must be able to weather any storm. There will be plenty of time for resting in the graveyard. Find a way to pull yourself up again and again and keep going. We all make many mistakes on the road. Change is a given and we never know what its newness will create.

Enlightenment 2

Travelers through the Cosmos

We must be free of external input to have our own inner link to universal truth. Deprogramming begins with that which was learned from family, friends, religion, society, school, television, radio, internet, and all not originating with you. Then there is separation from the 5 senses and their convincing view of reality. Each sense takes a slice of a given spectrum and instigates a solid image in the mind. We must not believe this to be reality. It is the imprint of the 3rd dimensional world. Simply put, our sense's view not our soul's. There is a higher perspective that reflects many different ways of perceiving. First we need quiet; then we need to listen.

Through this inner portal we can connect to source directly and have every question answered at once. Eventually questions cease because all is self evident at all times. We learn to look and see rather than seek and misconstrue. Sinking into that which already is, we open up to the force which breathes us and beats our heart in rhythm with nature. We are immersed in IT even as fish in the sea. Astral vibrancy is our ocean. Through releasing identity with self as it applies to circumstance we are able to restore our higher self to life in the body. Our soul has nothing to do with our era, society, or culture. We are space travelers on a journey of discovery; remember this and it begins.

Many seek alien contact and fail to realize that in a literal sense it is we who are the aliens. The human body is the meeting place for many creatures. Angels, demons, Sirians, Pleiadians, Orionids, reptilians, fairies, elves, trolls, and yet even more whom we dare not describe. There are also native terrestrials and the animal-humans who worked their way up the reincarnation ranks to become Earth's own cosmic contribution to the celestial game. There are the former Martians and Minervans (asteroid planet). Not to mention the visitors from our solar system's other planets as there is indeed life in the ether around the aura of our great giants. The good humored Saturnians, the heavenly Uranians, and the confident Jupiterians all drop by and even enter a body on occasion.

Get out of thinking of yourself as only a physical body. Find out about chakras if you haven't already and realize that you are a living constellation in the astral world – 4D. Your rainbow light body comes from the white light of the singularity – 5D. This is where we all meet and the 'I/eye' within you is the same 'I/eye' that is within me. This 'I/eye' is every

Enlightenment 2

'I/eye'…awareness itself. There is no monopoly on the eye as a symbol through which you can invoke this power. Any can utilize this tremendous archetype. One important way is as a means to contact the Sun and share Sol's Cosmic Mind through unifying with His 'I/eye'. It is surprising that Buddha didn't come right out and say it, but I suppose he was being crafty in his own way.

Another point to consider is that the living Earth's aura surrounds our own. At any time we can release the barriers which enforce separateness and allow the love of the mother to wash our burden away. We will hear passionate music and our heart will burst forth and rejoice in singing along. You will remember having heard it somewhere before…a long time ago, but it will be fresh, present, and new now. Joy will emanate from you and you will see that everything that everything that ever happened was just to get you here.

Ruminations of the Universe

Enlightenment 2
Infinite Consciousness amidst the Stars

Human beings are imitative creatures. We must take care not to get stuck in the replicating mechanism. The spark of divinity is in our originality. We can accrue knowledge of how to perform specific tasks and remain unbounded by the limitations of identifying with this information as ourselves. We are not facts figures or worldly achievements. We are the soul in a body having 3D experiences which we can enjoy while maintaining space and freedom.

Wisdom is awareness in the present and does not need to define everything in order to feel like it is doing something. Often people can not resist interjecting themselves into what is going on around them. Thinking that they are the center of the universe, they stir the waters everywhere they go. When the effects of their causes return to them they do not see that it was they who originated the happenings in the first place. Blaming others or even life itself, they lose touch with the goodness that is all around them.

Resting in the center of your being you can appreciate the beautiful reality which we are participants in. The interconnectedness of all things is not just a concept or a metaphor. We are literally being breathed by the same spirit. Our pulse dances with the heartbeat of the Earth. Every flower that blossoms reminds us of our own potential. Just beneath the surface the atoms flow fluidly across the cosmic graph, finding form for a time and then passing away.

Never forget the most basic truth. When you are walking around it is a planet in outer space upon which you trod. Your head is literally amidst the stars. Your home is not a house it is a galaxy. Four walls and a roof cannot contain an infinite consciousness. There is a reason for everything and you are never alone. We may isolate ourselves from time to time but when the ice melts there will always be friends both new and old to greet us. When we find happiness, the whole universe rejoices and all of humanity comes closer to lasting peace.

Enlightenment 2

Journey to the Center of Existence

We can be absolutely sure of something only to have the sands shift revealing another perspective. The key to evolution is accommodating change. Refusing to budge in your convictions can rally Will to your cause, but attempting to chart a course in contrast to the nature of the whole will result in strain, stress, and inevitably failure. One definition of success is the well-being cultivated from a given set of actions. There are many simple painters happier than rich tycoons. Friendship and a blissful heart lead to a contented and relaxed life.

Many forces on the outside will seek to coax you into chaos. Constant justifications will 'prove' that it is necessary for you to stir up trouble. Watch and see whether you are able to just be or if you are investing everything in a 'better' day that is yet to come. Cracking the psychic womb of expectations, we are able to get some space to breathe and let the moment reveal to us the next step on the path. Constantly we miss perfect solutions because we calculate our own desired circumstance.

Things may happen that we don't understand and we can curse the sky wailing, "Why did this happen to me!?" This expression of frustration is quite alright, but we must not get stuck in a repeating cycle of self-indulgence. Nothing can happen that wasn't meant to, and underneath every surface tapestry is exactly the right lesson. Consider what meaning an event has in the course of life's events. Also reflect deeper and see if the circumstance is trying to teach you a subtler quality of the soul. We must release the relentless demand for control in order for the universe to show us its more intricate secrets.

Be keenly aware of the influences around you. Are they helping or hindering your growth as a human? We all err on occasion, but some people are so full of bad habits that simply being near them will bring unfortunate variables your way. A nurturing friend can bring a multitude of blessings and raise your own idea of what you are able to do higher than you could have ever preconceived. Now imagine how far you can go if you align with the source of all friends and the very creator of the game you are playing.

We simultaneously exist as the fullness of our potential at once (SOUL) and that part in the body which has been actualized in the land of time. As we walk on, we attempt to synthesize these into one. When they have truly come together, the soul will be awake with full consciousness of its complete history through bodies and beyond. At the crossroads of divinity and terrestrial survival, we become a bridge that many can use to find their own connection to the center of existence.

Ruminations of the Universe

Enlightenment 2

The Universe Beckons You On

You may not see it, but it is there. Immersed in a mystery we swim for the freedom we already have. Invisible barriers made of nothing stand in our way. Traveling to the ends of the Earth we lose track of what we are searching for. Differentiating 'this' and 'that', we bite the Zen finger. Stirring up the mud we heed not Buddha's call to let it settle. Drinking contaminated water, we wonder why our stomach gets upset.

Resting on a rock in the middle of the night, our breath might finally catch us. Self-initiated rhythmic oscillations of atmosphere absorption keep our vessels sailing upon the seas of manifested life. Terrible failures and tremendous successes color the landscape, writing millions of unique and irreplaceable chapters of Existence. Nothing will ever disappear. The un-struck sound rings all at once. Letting go we gain the whole.

A circuitous route that might make Odysseus himself shudder, can lead the adventurous soul through countless shades of experience. The best preparation for the unknown is realizing that the currently known does not account for everything. Let the new bring magical rejuvenation. Be at once aware on your own, and able to open to the assistance that will arrive in the faces all around you. Take care to plant a good crop and the harvest will be abundant.

Change will occur again and again. Enjoy friends both old and new. Remember the myriad of relationships that you've had with your traveling companions through many lifetimes. There is no greater joy than the recovery of a beloved. The Universe itself expresses the origin of all Joy. The memory of your whole story is massive. Download all of your own soul's experiences and then one day you'll know all soul's collective experience. Being the one who sent forth Will into the World, this should be no surprise for you.

When the layers are at long last peeled away and sunlight can finally make it through the cracks to invigorate dormant potentialities, vibration is felt from the Source in every atom of the body and on into the astral realms. You connect with the music that has been all around you all along. It is the melody of home and the song wraps around you like a heart embrace. Longing to love you, the Universe beckons you on.

Enlightenment 2

Straight to the Source like a Rainbow Eagle

What's with all this present moment business? It is nothing less than the doorway to eternity. Phasing in fully to where you are, new dimensions open to you. No longer bound by linear time and the progression of events in the physical world, you slip into your astral body on your way to all encompassing awareness. What you see around you with the 5 senses is the surface…just the skin of existence. It is not conjecture or metaphoric to suggest that there are realms upon realms revealed in meditation. There are many ways to dabble, but if you want the truth, go straight to the Source.

You could contact a discarnate entity with little effort and they could easily fill you with messages that many would believe. In fact 'gods' of a sort are indeed there. Some are alien life forms and some exist as a different kind of being than what we are used to communicating with. Most on Earth are bound to perceiving themselves only in terrestrial context. The main thing that makes astral entities so enthralling is that they have a little higher perspective, out of the morass of mental confusion. Using your frame of reference they can send you thought forms from their location. But is it infinite truth?

Often it is said that the greatest danger to a seeker is to get their first few occult powers and lose themselves in the wielding of these over those who know not their light heritage. It takes discipline knowing that you are the representative of the divine to avoid these tantalizing pitfalls. There is so much more to know. We can assimilate telepathy, astral vision, astral travel, dream consciousness, future-prophesy, and creative freedom the likes of which make you feel like a rainbow eagle soaring through the sky. Also you will see in others many things: past lives, animal totems, and mythological eventualities.

At some point you will be beyond it all; a giant eye in the sky that can at any time send intention through the myriad of talents given by the Universe. One great reason not to get lost in messages from the creatures hanging around in the 4th dimensional astral realms is because it gives them position over us. In fact our destiny lies beyond even these heavenly places. You see, these beings in the ether are not flawless. They are still where they are because they have yet to master all desires and attachments. Buddha would simply wink at their hi-jinks. That's why he is such a beauty.

Enlightenment 2

Cracking the Code of Manifestation

Never worry about the rejuvenation of ideas in this Creation. Time and Space are elusive. Sometimes perceptions shift and seem a bit longer or shorter. The fountain of inspiration never fails to bring forth the new. To have a similar occurrence within you and experience what God does is no small order. Can anybody do it? Of course! But who among you is willing to let go enough to facilitate the happening? How we love our comforts, habits, and security. Do you love the adventure of Life more? The whispers of the Heart will show you the way if you have courage and the will to proceed further.

God is Life and Love is Spirit. Personality becomes Individuality becomes Universality. Then the stars reside in you. They are your body. The inherent lines between points of light create a cosmic graph of energy. We disperse into this and recover all experience from all beings. Every potential taking place on every dimension is seen simultaneously as one. Before manifestation plays out through the realms it is Intent in the Intelligence of Existence. We can leave our role in the playing out of events and skip right back to the thought that begat it all in the first place.

The Sun gives birth to planets which conceive of moons who establish moods in which young couples make Love on sultry summer nights. Maybe some of you have remembered our Earth's moon, Luna. She has seen us through many lifetimes. Artemis I run with you. She is a link for continuity in our process of piecing together the Soul's experience. Sometimes a shock is needed to break through the density; sometimes just the changing of a season is enough. A catchy tune can reach your depths and transform your being. A pretty picture can bring a smile that warms your cockles.

So many have come and gone. What happens to the potential in a human that is unrevealed? It exists with all other possibilities as one in the idea, but the experience gained from manifestation and reflection is not accrued. Therefore new phenomenon will be presented again and again that will work on those same areas trying to elicit the response which will actualize the next step in one's progression. Every moment is the master if we look deeply enough and have the right attitude. Everything in front of you right now is a code that can be cracked.

In dreams and in waking life our guides and friends share our journey. Try to avoid making

Enlightenment 2

mistakes that can not be taken back. Slow this whole thing down and you will not be disappointed. There may be bills to pay and games to play, but there are also deep truths to be understood. This is a part of life that isn't always bantered about in public, but it is there. Many have attained to realizations so profound that they could never be preconceived. The soundless clap resounds abundantly. The goose is no longer in the bottle; in fact he is taking a gander at the myriad of forms in the flesh and marveling at their beauty.

Ruminations of the Universe

Enlightenment 2

The Interconnection of All things

Nature has many ways to express itself. Infinite permutations compose a piece called life. Everywhere you can see the artistic hand of the creator. Even this sentence would not be possible without prana invigorating the medulla and connecting the writer to the Source. Whether it is a painting by Michelangelo or a morning sunrise, anything infused with the Holy Spirit of creativity can become the catalyst for awakening.

It is said that Lao Tzu became enlightened by watching a leaf fall from a tree. There is also a story that Sir Isaac Newton defined gravity after an apple fell on his head. Buddha arrived watching the stars underneath the bodhi tree. In these moments, the mind was not crowding out the experience of the present. The more you think, the less you are here and now.

All creative works can be enjoyed in their own right, but looking even deeper you encounter that which gave rise to the phenomenon in the first place. Being in the world of man, we lose touch with the brilliance underlying all manifestation. Imagine what it was like before the busy cities, serious jobs, and artificial superstructures. It is still like that if we can slow down, listen, and open the door within to perceive in another way.

No matter what you create, even if it is the most beautifully poetic work of art in existence, it is not an end. Creation is an ongoing experiment and each form is an indicator towards the light within. On the surface we are individuals and in spirit we are one. Serving the flow of Tao can be the link to your own awareness of the interconnected nature of all things great and small.

Enlightenment 2

Astral Love Frequencies

One cannot say for certain which direction the flow will release their potential. Preconceptions cause the ache of unfulfilled expectations. Yesterday slips through now to become tomorrow and….gone. Somehow we are able to catch a little bit of what happens. Ponder these events and you might discover many things; none of them will be the ultimate answer as that is only realized when humming…running…singing….

When a cycle turns you can sense the breath of change bringing you to where you could never have imagined. Sometimes fun and sometimes scary….nonetheless….we can grow from every experience if our attitude is aligned with this concept. It is not wrong in any way to project strength. Aggressiveness is a completely different phenomenon. You can have an honorable power that deals with circumstances courageously.

It is baffling…the pockets of magic that move around ready to dance you into the absurd. Watch with the eye and you reflect perfectly what occurs. Smile, in your mastery you are awareness and joy. You and your father become one and for a moment you feel the benediction and bliss of the heavenly host. Singing alleluia they praise

God over and over again, not due to duty, but because it is their inherent nature to Love.

Sleeping through much of what occurs, the somnolent miss. Each moment is a beauty when you understand the miracle of being alive. Everything is extra. Fighting for trinkets, the naughty peoples have gotten themselves into trouble. Something in them seeks chaos and disaster…it is because they haven't learned the subtle benefits of peace. Nothing happening can be wonderful…..ahhhh…..nothing to disturb.

Enlightenment 2

The End of Suffering

Nothing seems so simple as seeing something right in front of your face. Some kind of light beam has penetrated this place. I can no longer use the language of the land. There is something else to understand.

High humming and a sigh of relief. The end of suffering; the end of belief.

And yet it goes on dangerously close to the wicked path… Nary yet a whisper. Everybody becomes discorporate. How else to give yourself room to move? Something has happened to the outside world.

Why do they creep restrictions? Why do they heap indignations?

It isn't interesting if it stays the same. It isn't funny if it ends up with a hassle. You know how bad it sucks to be inconvenienced. Damn the world, get me to the front of the line. Naw…wait. I got 5 minutes. Let me look at the tabloids.

Isn't it strange how some people can't cry? Guess they don't want to fly.

By now you must have realized that linearly is not the method to be provoked by this demonstration of wits. Mark Twain himself might think, "Hmmm….the kid's got something here." You remember his whiskers don't you?

The past isn't gone, it's everywhere. Heal now or forgive yourself later.

I did it all for you my beloveds. There are realities left that are benevolent and relentlessly working for the good of all humanity. Even when we fall we learn something. The ability to carry on is one of the true essentials.

O Lord Give them eyes to see, emotions to feel, and empathy for each other.

THERE IS A WHOLE OTHER UNIVERSE JUST BEHIND THE ONE YOU USED TO KNOW. THERE IS A WHOLE OTHER UNIVERSE JUST BEHIND THE ONE YOU USED TO KNOW. THERE WAS A MOLE THAT JUMPED IN A HOLE AND FOUND THERE A SCROLL. HE UNROLLED IT AND IT SAID, "THERE IS A WHOLE OTHER UNIVERSE JUST BEHIND THE ONE YOU USED TO KNOW."

Enlightenment 2

An Experiment in Integrity

If Buckminster Fuller's life was an experiment to see what one man could do for the good of all humanity, I suppose you could say that mine is an experiment to see what happens when you actually live integrity every moment of every day. It brings you endless matters to attend to in that the patterns around you are full of compromise. You can not be caught napping for a split second or else you will be drawn in to the enticing temptations of temporary gain.

Living the truth of who you are does not mean things will always be easy. It is an approach that keeps you whole so you can be relaxed and tune in to the higher vibrations of the universe. So many deceivers cross your path and they all have something to sell. Sometimes subtle and sometimes overt, the psychic map is full of astral land mines. There is certainly no guarantee that a journey once begun will be completed. It is much more likely that you will falter.

The more you give, the more you will gain. This is not in material possessions, but in spiritual energy. As Barry Long says, Love is the currency of the spirit and Money is the currency of the world. If you want things, you will be of the world, if you want Love, you will seek refuge in spirit. Then, things will come and go but your peace will remain undisturbed. This is practice in preparation for when you have to give up your prize possessions of the Body and the Mind.

The Body/Mind complex is simply a vehicle of external perception. Your soul can easily shed these limitations and through this exquisite vehicle exhibit spiritual qualities. These are not holy-moly displays of moral judgment, but true grace and fluidity in manifesting moment to moment reality. Sending a healthy glow to the world, the whole is benefited immensely just be your being here. Each of our programs will go into the human matrix. If you design your own as such, it will influence beneficently evermore.

Enlightenment 2

Sunshine Sutra

Let light shine from within to without.

Questions need not arise; there is self-evidency in truth.

Happiness is a by-product of peace.

Come down from the mountain and sit for a spell.

You have much to do; none of it is consequential.

What is here is what you seek.

Explanations can not give you the taste of wine.

Drink deeply and know; the inebriation of spirit delights.

Shower blessings to friend and foe.

Buddha's wisdom is as simple as a smile.

Dark forces flee before the candle; at once all is revealed.

There is no time and this is the place.

Patience is necessary to foster and enjoy growth.

Impetuousness blocks Tao; how can a dammed river flow?

Easy and free like a bird in the tree, we see.

Keep thinking if you wish yourself confusion.

Neither this nor that nor the other thing; all mind stuff is an excuse.

Distractions do not bother a disciplined disciple.

Shed layer upon layer of your burden.

Let go of tightly gripped grime; fear becomes fun.

The vivaciousness of life perpetually amazes.

Try hard and then give it a rest.

After all stones have been turned there will be rain.

When the sun comes out, you will be a rainbow.

Also by Christopher Moors

Take a journey through the astral realms. Awaken the truth encoded deep within your DNA. Open up to a cosmology you always hoped could be.

Mission of the Creative Cosmos

To invoke the unity of Eastern Wisdom and Western Art.

To assist in the evolving consciousness and destiny of humanity.

To make this information available to the widest possible audience.

http://www.creativecosmos.org

www.ingramcontent.com/pod-product-compliance
Lightning Source LLC
Chambersburg PA
CBHW070635160426
43194CB00009B/1466